A BLESSED AND HIGHLY FAVORED LIFE

Rising to the High Calling of
Accepting God's Purpose for Your Life

Dr. R. Timothy Jones

sermonto**book**
.com

Sermon To Book
www.sermontobook.com

A Blessed And Highly Favored Life / Dr. R. Timothy Jones
ISBN-13: 9780692532775
ISBN-10: 0692532773

This book is dedicated to three awesome women who have remarkably blessed my life:

My bride, Sherbrina Trammel Jones

My mother, Thelma Lee Walker Jones

My secretary of many years, Carla Mims Shepard

CONTENTS

A Note from the Author

Hello, and thank you for purchasing *A Blessed and Highly Favored Life*.

Accompanying each chapter of the book is a set of reflective questions. These workbook sections serve as a practical tool to help you get the most out of the book— to help you truly learn how to lead a blessed life from the stories and examples of several remarkable biblical women.

Each workbook section includes questions for discussion or reflection as well as a summary geared toward practical application. I recommend you go through these sections with a pen in order to write your thoughts in the areas provided.

You are welcome to go through the questions by yourself, with a friend, or with a study group. Regardless, it is my hope that you enjoy the book thoroughly and grow from the experience!

CHAPTER ONE

A Blessed and Highly Favored Life

The angel went to her and said, "Greetings, you who are
highly favored! The Lord is with you." — **Luke 1:28 (NIV)**

A couple thousand years ago, life would have seemed
humdrum in the backwater town of Nazareth, especially
for a teenage girl like Mary. In this village where nothing
much ever happened, all she ever got to do was help her
mother look after the family. She'd cook and sweep, and
once or twice a day she'd walk down to the well.

Mary was probably only thirteen or fourteen, but her
parents had mapped out her life for her. They'd arranged
for her to marry a suitable guy with a solid reputation,
and soon enough Mary would know the burdens of
running a household just as her mother had done. Babies
would probably arrive quickly, and eventually, if all

went well, Mary would one day bounce grandchildren on her lap too. That was her grand purpose, as far as she knew.

How little she *did* know!

As she did her daily chores, Mary often thought about her fiancé, a man that her parents had considered a suitable choice for her. They said he would be good to her. He was a carpenter—good with his hands, kind hearted, and well spoken of. He traced his family line back to King David, too. Many girls had done a lot worse, Mary decided, and there was comfort in routine.

Then one day, Mary's predictable life was shattered by the arrival of an unexpected visitor.

"Congratulations, highly favored lady!" said the visitor, whose name was Gabriel. "The Lord is with you, and you are blessed among women!"

To be blessed and highly favored is simply to be used by God for His purpose.

Do you know what it means to be blessed and highly favored? First let's be clear about what it does *not* mean. It's not about privilege, power, or prominence. Nor is it about position, possessions, or prestige. It's not being able to claim whatever you can name. It has nothing to do with being above versus being below; the head versus the tail; the lender versus the borrower. It has nothing to with what you have, who you know, what you drive, or where you live. It's not even about health and wealth.

To be blessed and highly favored is simply to be used by God for His purpose.

Now, if being greeted in person by an angel weren't alarming enough for Mary, Gabriel had still more to say, anticipating her distress.

"Don't be frightened, Mary," he said, "for God has decided to wonderfully bless you! Very soon now you will become pregnant and have a baby boy and you are to name him Jesus."

This child, he went on, would be called the Son of the living God.

And this was good news?

We cannot blame Mary for feeling anxious. She could not imagine how God was going to pull this off.

In hindsight, we know it was. But at that moment, Mary was not so sure. Emotions swirled around her head as she tried to fathom the implications of what she was hearing. Who would believe her? She had been brought up as a virtuous Jewish girl. And virtuous Jewish girls did not get pregnant outside of marriage. Not if they valued their lives. To be fatally stoned for an illicit relationship did not bear thinking about.

We cannot blame Mary for feeling anxious. She could not imagine how God was going to pull this off.

Mary and Joseph were engaged to be married, but she was being asked to put her plans on the line, her reputation on the line, her body on the line, and ultimately her own life on the line.

"How could this possibly be?" Mary asked, trembling. "I'm not even married!"

Gabriel answered that the Holy Spirit would come upon her and overshadow her, adding that every promise from God would surely come true.

Mary needed this reassurance. Did her Creator whisper in her ear words similar to the ones he had spoken to Jeremiah, centuries earlier?

I know the plans I have for you ... They are plans for good and not for evil, to give you a future and a hope. — **Jeremiah 29:11 (TLB)**

That verse was a reminder that nothing was impossible with God. *Could the living God really have a glorious purpose for her?*

Mary had nothing. No expensive chariot, no six–figure income, no higher education. But she was called blessed and highly favored because of what God was planning to do through her. Clearly, God saw something in Mary that no one else had seen, including Joseph and Mary herself. She wouldn't have made it into the *Who's Who* of Galilee. She had no title, no treasure, no talent, no special seat in the sanctuary. She had no dollars, diamonds, or degrees.

But the Lord was with Mary, and that made all the difference. If God were for her, who could be against her (Romans 8:31, NIV)?

There was a long pause as she swallowed hard.

"I am the Lord's servant," Mary said, quietly, "and I'm willing to do whatever He wants."

Divine Intervention

At the beginning of the story, we see nothing remarkable about Mary. She and Joseph were ordinary people living in a hick town, far from the bustle of the capital, Jerusalem. Joseph was a practical man who just wanted to live happily ever after with his young wife. On the verge of their marriage, he and Mary were not signing up for any drama, and were certainly not expecting God to deliver it.

Can you imagine Joseph's feelings at first? He would have been heartbroken by what was happening to Mary. He would have anticipated the gossip, the misunderstandings, the criticism, the slurs, and the innuendoes that would be voiced within their close-knit community.

Understandably, he had issues with what God was doing in his fiancée's life. In fact, he planned to divorce her quietly and move off the scene. God had to accost him dramatically to regain his trust.

Upheavals are never part of anyone's plan. But have you noticed how God has a tendency to interrupt our designs?

Let's face it. For most of us, God has not been constantly on our minds since childhood. For much of our lives, we operate under our own ability, doing life in a way that seems to make sense for us. The fact that we become believers at all is proof of God's intervention.

Have we ever thought of thanking God for interrupting our plans? We have prayed "Your will be done on earth as it is in heaven" countless times. But have we ever considered that what God may have for us is better than what we think we want?

The turning point in our lives is when we decide to live by favor rather than fear.

It's easy to praise God for the things we've received. But what about the things we've missed? We may not have many gifts under the Christmas tree, but have we escaped cancer? We may not have much in the bank, but do we have health? May we live long enough to thank God for all the times He has said "no" to us. One day we'll thank him for all the folk who turned us down.

The turning point in our lives is when we decide to live by favor rather than fear.

Fear says, "I can't get through this situation." Favor says, "And we know that in all things God works together for the good of those who love him, who have been called according to his purpose" (Romans 8:28, NIV). Fear says, "They're out to get me," but favor says, "No weapon forged against you will prevail, and you will refute every tongue that accuses you" (Isaiah 54:17, NIV).

The blessed and highly favored life sometimes goes against the grain of conventional wisdom. In our story, God uses an unlikely place: Nazareth. Then He uses an unlikely person: a young and unlearned peasant girl. What God did in the life of Mary causes us to rethink what it means to be prosperous.

The blessed and highly favored life is not really about who we are, but whose we are. It is not about externals but what God is doing in our life internally.

"...no weapon forged against you will prosper, and you will refute every tongue that accuses you. This is the heritage of the servants of the LORD, *and this is their vindication from me," declares the* LORD. — **Isaiah 54:17 (NIV)**

In short, "Quit trying to figure me out, and learn how to trust."

That's why the angel told Mary not to fear. Thank God she didn't allow her doubts to prevail, for she recognized that God's favor would ultimately lead to His accomplishing His purpose in her.

There will always be things we don't comprehend. But we're not called to understand. We're called to believe. If the Lord can feed five thousand—not including the women and children—He can feed you. If He can get Moses out of the Red Sea, He can get you out of your dilemma. If He can get the boys out of the fiery furnace, He can get you out of whatever's keeping you trapped.

Mary saw herself as the maidservant of God.

"I may not understand it," she told herself, "but let it be. If you want to use me to bring the Savior into the world, I'll birth Him in a cattle barn; I'll lay Him in a cow's manger; I'll raise Him in my husband's carpentry shop. If you want to use me to bring the Son of God into this place, I'm ready."

Reality is More Than Appearance

We, like Mary, might not measure up to society's expectations. But if God is with us, we don't have to fulfill anyone else's criteria. We may be nothing to look at by the world's standards, but God tells us we are fearfully and wonderfully made, created in His image and likeness. He tells us we're the salt of the earth and the light of the world, a holy nation and a royal priesthood. That's good news!

We might be poor, like Mary. But the best things in life cannot be expressed on a balance sheet. Even if there is money in the bank, it will eventually leave us or we will leave it. The truth is, we cannot take it with us.

I love the story of the rich man who refused to believe this. At his funeral, the people noticed thousands of dollars stashed beside him in his coffin. That's when an astute fellow announced, "Tell you what, I'll take all this money and write him a check instead. If he can spend all this money where he's going, he can surely cash a check as well."

The other day I was watching a CPA work on my church's accounts and prepare a summary. I wondered how he was going to convey joy on that balance sheet. Of course, that wasn't what he was looking for, but Sunday by Sunday a heap of joy was being produced—including testimonies of transformation and deliverance. And none of it could be quantified.

Things are rarely what they seem.

An Italian politician once noticed an elderly woman who visited a cathedral every day. For years she turned up daily to pray before a statue of the Virgin Mary. One day the politician spoke to an elderly priest about it, commenting on the marvelous faith this woman had.

"Don't be deceived by what you see," the priest told him. "Many years ago, when the sculptor was making that statue, he needed a model to pose for him, so he hired a beautiful young woman. That elderly lady was that young woman. She isn't coming to pray. She is coming to worship what she used to be."

Here was a sad woman for whom appearance was more important than reality.

Elizabeth

There was a second woman in Mary's life who was blessed and highly favored—and she had a miracle pregnancy, too. This was Mary's relative Elizabeth, whom we read about at the beginning of Luke 1. In fact, she was already six months pregnant with John the Baptist when Mary received her miraculous visit from the angel.

Why was Elizabeth's pregnancy such a miracle? Well, first of all, she was getting up in years. Not only had she never borne children, but her time for childbearing had run out. It seemed to be all over for Elizabeth and her elderly husband.

But six months prior, God had put John in Elizabeth's womb. And when He did, Elizabeth hid herself for five months because she knew most people wouldn't understand. People always talked. And if tongues wagged when a *young* woman got pregnant, what would they say about an *elderly* woman?

But notice something else about Elizabeth. She was the only person Mary talked to about her situation. Why did she trust Elizabeth with her secret? Well, the Bible tells us Elizabeth was filled with the Holy Spirit, and before Mary even opened her mouth, her aunt told her, "Honey, you are blessed." The older woman had spiritual discernment, and Mary knew it.

When you start talking about what God's doing in your life, you can be sure some people won't understand.

Not everybody can handle a blessed and highly favored life. When you start talking about what God's doing in your life, you can be sure some people won't understand. They'll shoot holes in your dreams and they'll tell you what you can't do. But if they rain on your parade, just tell them: "I know it's pouring, baby, but I'm still going on my picnic!"

And remember what happened next? John the Baptist, in the second trimester of his mother's pregnancy, danced for joy. When he sensed the presence of his cousin Jesus, he leapt in his mother's womb (Luke 1:41).

Then Mary offered up some praise of her own.

"My soul glorifies the Lord," she said.

When God is calling us to do something that we've never done before and cannot do by ourselves, when we're backed into a corner with no obvious way out, we can thank God for making us a candidate for a miracle.

Is it time to open your heart to what God might do *through* you? Mary had nothing, but she was available to God. Elizabeth was barren, but she too was open to the Lord's purpose. Are you ready for a blessed and highly favored life? The turning point in Mary's life came once she began to see herself as God saw her.

It should be your turning point, too.

WORKBOOK

Chapter One Questions

Question: Are you willing to serve God? How could you put everything on the line to do what He has asked you to do?

_____

_____

_____

_____

_____

_____

_____

_____

_____

_____

_____

_____

_____

_____

_____

Question: Have you ever thanked God for interrupting your plans? When has His interruption in your life caused your circumstances to come together for good?

_____

_____

_____

_____

_____

_____

_____

_____

_____

_____

_____

_____

_____

_____

Question: How can your experience encourage someone else?

_____

_____

_____

Summary: The turning point in our lives is once we decide to live by favor rather than fear. Quit trying to figure God out, and learn how to trust Him. The blessed and highly favored life is not about externals, but about what God is doing in our lives internally. When God is calling us to do something that we've never done before, we can thank God for making us candidates for a miracle. Open your heart to what God might do through you.

Notes

_____

_____

_____

_____

_____

_____

_____

_____

_____

_____

_____

_____

_____

_____

_____

_____

_____

_____

_____

_____

_____

_____

_____

CHAPTER TWO

The Day Her Life Changed Forever

And suddenly, a woman who had a flow of blood for twelve years came from behind and touched the hem of His garment. For she said to herself, "If only I may touch His garment, I shall be made well." But Jesus turned around, and when He saw her He said, "Be of good cheer, daughter; your faith has made you well." And the woman was made well from that hour. — **Matthew 9:20-22 (NKJV)**

Our world celebrates the lifestyles of the rich and the famous. We're fascinated by people whose reputations precede them. But this chapter is about the people in Scripture whom I call the nameless notables. Though we don't know their names, we know their stories. The Bible invites us to feel their pain and to participate in their challenges as if they were our own. Their experiences remind us of the highs and lows, the ups and downs, and the ins and outs of our own lives.

The unnamed woman in our text helps us see our frustrations through the lens of our faith, rather than our fears. She illustrates how to practice perseverance in the face of pain. She teaches us that even when we're helpless, we're never hopeless. She demonstrates what it means to operate according to our courage, rather than our condition.

She had been struggling for twelve years with an issue of blood. It was a gynecological crisis that had crippled her. It had made her ceremonially unclean, according to Levitical law, so she was alienated from society and banned from the temple. She had tried everything, spent all she had, but things had only gotten worse. Yet, as she grew weaker, her faith grew stronger.

We all have issues. For the woman in our text, it was a blood issue. Richard "Dimples" Field sang it best: "If it ain't one thing, it's another!"

This story is about a woman whose life was changed forever. Her story should give us hope for our hurts, and courage for our conditions. Her encounter with Christ should motivate us to a fresh perseverance in the face of pain. Like this woman, one of the nameless notables, may we allow our faith to conquer our fear.

We all have issues. For the woman in our text, it was a blood issue. Richard "Dimples" Field sang it best: "If it ain't one thing, it's another!"[1]

Your issue may be spiritual—maybe you cannot feel the presence of God. Or you may have a mental issue—perhaps your mind is disturbed. When your heart is beating but broken, it's an emotional issue. When you look good but feel bad, it's probably a physical issue.

It's a marital issue when neither you nor your spouse seem to be trying anymore. It's a domestic issue when your house is not a home. It's a financial issue when there's too much month left at the end of the money. It's a social issue when you've found true enemies and fake friends.

It's not the size of the dog in the fight, it's the size of the fight in the dog.

What's your particular issue today? Is it a burden God has not yet lifted? Is it a question that is yet to be answered? Is it a problem you cannot seem to solve? Is it a stronghold that has not yet been broken? Is it a sin you don't believe God will forgive? Is it a loved one who needs to be delivered? Is it a breakthrough that has yet to come? A sickness God has not yet healed? A bill that needs to be paid?

The woman in our text had every reason to give up. She'd done all she could, gone from doctor to doctor, specialist to specialist. She'd used up all her resources, tapped out her savings. Perhaps the doctor had released her to hospice care. For all practical purposes, it was over. The fat lady was clearing her throat to sing.

But a football coach said it best: "It's not the size of the dog in the fight, it's the size of the fight in the dog."

I cannot help everything that happens to me, but I can choose what to internalize. I cannot help what everybody calls me, but I can decide what I answer to. I cannot help everything I go through, but I've made up in my mind, "I'm going to trust in the Lord!" The woman in our text had the issue, but the issue did not have her.

Let's look at the process here.

From Disease to Destitution

Generally, when we talk about disease, we want to talk about cancer or some other physiological tragedy. But disease is spelled *dis-ease*. A disease is a person or thing that disturbs the *ease* in your life. When your tooth aches, you visit a dentist; when your stomach hurts, you go to a gastroenterologist; when your foot is the problem, you see a podiatrist. But when your mind is disturbed or your heart is broken, only God (plus a little time) will heal.

This woman's disease has turned into destitution, that place where she had nothing left. Mark offers deeper insight into the woman's situation. He tells us she had suffered many things from physicians. She'd been to the health food store. She'd tried herbs and minerals. She may have gotten her palms read. She'd tried one doctor after another, one clinic after another, one appointment after another, one specialist after another, yet she'd only grown worse.

What do you do when things get worse? I've lived long enough to know there are times when things will get worse before they get better. Have you ever felt like you were walking through a valley?

The key is to keep walking, because at some point you'll get through it.

From Destitution to Desperation

It seemed this woman had nothing left but her faith. But God can do more with our faith than we can do with our finances. Sometimes God waits until our finances are exhausted because then we are *forced* to exercise our faith. When we are reduced to nothing, we discover we still have God. And if we have Him, we have more than enough. Faith can keep us after the resources have vanished.

How do you react when you have nobody and nothing left?

Trust in the LORD with all your heart and lean not on your own understanding; in all your ways acknowledge him, and he will make your paths straight. — **Proverbs 3:5-6 (NIV)**

"Here comes Jesus," said this desperate woman. "What do I have to do?"

Remember, according to Levitical law, she was ceremonially unclean. She wasn't supposed to touch anybody, and nobody was supposed to touch her.

"According to the law, I can't touch Jesus," she told herself, "but there's no law that says I can't touch the hem of His garment!"

From Desperation to Deliverance

I like this woman, because her conviction is greater than her condition. When her back is against the wall, she says things like, "I can do all this through him who gives me strength" (Philippians 4:13, NIV).

She should have thrown in the towel. But she believed God "will keep in perfect peace those whose minds are steadfast, because they trust in [Him]" (Isaiah 26:3, NIV).

She had nothing, but she knew God would meet all her needs "from his riches in glory because of what Christ Jesus has done for us" (Philippians 4:19, TLB). She had nothing left, but I hear her saying, "I lift up my eyes to the hills. From where does my help come? My help comes from the LORD, who made heaven and earth" (Psalm 121:1-2, ESV).

She could lose sleep over what other folk were saying about her, but she was rejoicing over what Jesus was saying to her. Listen to her words: "If only I can just touch the hem of his garment I'll be made well."

And see how Jesus spoke to her heart before He spoke to her health. "Be of good cheer!" he says. In other words, "Shout, and shout right now! Don't worry about how it looks!"

If the Lord says "shout," He obviously knows something we don't know. So if He says shout, then shout! We've simply got to learn how to operate according to our courage, not according to our condition. Plato once said, "Courage is knowing what not to fear." All we need to do is allow what God has put in us to handle what's happening to us. The woman's health had failed, but her hope remained.

Whatever you do, don't lose hope. In a London art gallery, there is a painting by George Frederick Watts (1817-1904). It's simply entitled *Hope*. In it, a blindfolded woman sits atop the world. She's oblivious to both the star above her and the world of darkness and gloom below. She has a broken lyre with one string. Perhaps in her dejection she is thinking about the broken lyre and making whatever music she can with that one string. That's hope. She's isolated, without vision, and barefoot. Despite the title, she appears to be on the edge of despair.

Many scholars, critics, philosophers and theologians have pondered the title of this painting. *Hope,* Mr. Watts? How can you call this *Hope*? Where is hope in such a dismal work of art? The woman has only a broken lyre with one string.

When you decide to make whatever music you can with all you have left, that's *hope*.

James Weldon Johnson (1871–1928) once wrote these inspiring words:

Lift every voice and sing

Till earth and heaven ring

Ring with the harmonies of Liberty

Let our rejoicing rise

High as the list'ning skies

Let it resound loud as the rolling sea

Sing a song full of the faith

That the dark past has taught us

Sing a song full of the hope

That the present has brought us

Facing the rising sun

Of our new day begun

Let us march on

Till victory is won[2]

Remember, the woman in our story had lived twelve years with her condition. Her miracle of healing was preceded by her miracle of perseverance.

Have you ever wondered how you made it? Do you ever look back and wonder how you got through? The truth is, some of the stuff you've been through should have taken you out, but you're still here. You've had some tough times, but you're still here. People look at you and wonder why you haven't lost your mind. If others had been through what you've been through, they would have thrown in the towel long ago. They saw you smiling on the outside, but didn't have a clue what was happening on the inside. They've seen your glory without knowing your story.

Celebrate perseverance! As Paul put it, "We are hard pressed on every side, but not crushed; perplexed, but not in despair; persecuted, but not abandoned; struck down, but not destroyed" (2 Corinthians 4:8-9, NIV).

WORKBOOK

Chapter Two Questions

Question: Have you struggled with something for a while, now or in the past? How did you make it through—or how can you continue onward, if you are still facing this struggle?

_____

_____

_____

_____

_____

_____

_____

_____

_____

_____

_____

_____

_____

_____

_____

Question: Consider the Watts painting and the quote from James Weldon Johnson in this chapter. How do these images and words apply to a struggle you are facing now? Where you do you find your hope?

_____

_____

_____

_____

_____

_____

_____

_____

_____

_____

_____

_____

_____

_____

Question: When has your perseverance in the face of serious challenges affected others in the past? How did they respond to your courage?

_____

_____

_____

_____

_____

_____

_____

_____

_____

_____

_____

_____

_____

_____

_____

Summary: We all have issues, but Richard "Dimples" Field sang it best: "If it ain't one thing, it's another!" The key is to keep walking, because at some point we will get through our troubles. In the meantime, we must learn to operate according to our courage, not according to our condition, and to see our frustrations through faith, not fear. In this way, we will let people see our glory even without knowing our story.

Notes

_____

_____

_____

_____

_____

_____

_____

_____

_____

_____

_____

_____

_____

_____

_____

_____

_____

_____

_____

_____

_____

_____

CHAPTER THREE

Got Self-Esteem?

When the LORD saw that Leah was unloved, he enabled her to have children, but Rachel could not conceive. So Leah became pregnant and gave birth to a son. She named him Reuben, for she said, "The LORD has noticed my misery, and now my husband will love me." She soon became pregnant again and gave birth to another son. She named him Simeon, for she said, "The LORD heard that I was unloved and has given me another son." Then she became pregnant a third time and gave birth to another son. He was named Levi, for she said, "Surely this time my husband will feel affection for me, since I have given him three sons!" Once again Leah became pregnant and gave birth to another son. She named him Judah, for she said, "Now I will praise the LORD!" And then she stopped having children. — **Genesis 29:31-35 (NLT)**

There is no value more significant than self-value. If we do not value ourselves, we begin to see ourselves as inferior or incompetent when compared to others. Failure to value ourselves leads to insecurity, and we long for the approval of others. We feel good about ourselves only when other people feel good about us.

The story of Leah and her less-than-perfect marriage with Jacob illustrates what self-value is. It's no secret that Leah was not the girl of Jacob's dreams. She was never the apple of his eye. Their relationship was at best complicated, but it teaches us what it means to see ourselves through the eyes of God rather than through the eyes of others.

If we don't value ourselves, we cannot maintain a healthy relationship with anybody else. Remember, Jesus taught us to love our neighbours *as* we love ourselves. So it's okay to love ourselves!

In passing, I want to say there's nothing wrong with being single. You should be able to walk into a restaurant and say with pride, "Table for one." Understand that you can enjoy life by yourself. Fly yourself to Jamaica. Stretch out on the beach by yourself. Swim in the Caribbean by yourself. *Pay* yourself. You are whole in and of yourself, and you are worth it.

If somebody asks, "Where are you going?"
tell them, "I'm going out with me.*"*

You need to value yourself, even if nobody else values you. There's nothing wrong with you being your number one fan. Get up in the morning and get dressed. Put on your Sunday clothes in the morning. If somebody asks, "Where are you going?" tell them, "I'm going out with *me*." Put on your face and comb your hair. Do it for *you.* Look in the mirror and say, "Woohoo! Didn't God do a miracle! Just look at what He made!"

When we fail to value ourselves, we live through substitutes. We may crave status symbols, but it's possible to drive a Mercedes-Benz in the wrong direction! Nor does the price of a house make it a home. We can light the fire and the house can still feel cold. We may live through competition, trying to outdo other people so we can feel better about ourselves. We may crave approval, because we can only feel good about ourselves when others like us.

Low self-esteem is generally caused by the abuse, the absence, or the apathy of a significant person in your life.

Then there are envy and jealousy. How would you like to take your life to a whole new level? If so, I dare you to praise God for what He's done *for somebody else.* Tell the Lord, "This wasn't my year, but the reason I'm shouting is because I've watched you bless my sister and I've watched you bless my brother. And if you can do it for him in the year just past, there's no telling what you can do for me in the year ahead!"

Low self-esteem is generally caused by the abuse, the absence, or the apathy of a significant person in your life. Many people struggling with low self-esteem were failed as children. If you're a parent now, please don't make the same mistake with your own children. They need your time, and it's time you won't ever have again. Make whatever sacrifices you have to make to be there with and for them.

But the next morning, he realized it wasn't Rachel at all. It was her sister, Leah!

Let's look at what was going on in our text. Jacob met Rachel, the girl of his dreams. Rachel was beautiful, but her older sister, Leah, was not. The Bible says that when Jacob met Rachel, who was his cousin, he kissed her and broke into tears. So his Uncle Laban, Rachel's father, invited him into his home and gave him a job. But he recognized he needed to compensate Jacob for his work.

"Tell you what," said Jacob. "I've been looking at your daughter Rachel."

So he agreed to work seven years in order to marry Rachel, and after seven years he married who he thought was the woman of his dreams. But the next morning, he realized it wasn't Rachel at all. It was her sister, Leah!

Not surprisingly, Jacob confronted Laban in some anger.

"Let me tell you something, nephew," Laban responded smoothly. "In these parts, the baby girl doesn't get married first. But I'll tell you what, if you agree to work seven more years for me, you can have Rachel as well."

So Jacob worked seven long years to get Rachel and seven more to keep her. But here's the thing: verse 30 says *Jacob loved Rachel more than he loved Leah.*

Can you picture Leah's misery? It began with her name, which literally meant *disgusting.* It meant "to grieve" or "to make weary." How would you feel if your mother named you *disgusting?* Leah was not attractive. Verse 17 tells us she had weak eyes but Rachel was lovely in form and beauty.

It got worse. Jacob married Leah on a misunderstanding, so she ended up married to a man who loved someone else. And the other woman just happened to be her baby sister. What a mess!

Why didn't Jacob hear her? Because he wasn't listening.

But here's the thing: Rachel might have been loved by Jacob, but Leah was loved by God. So Leah began to have children, and the story of her misery is written in the names she gave them.

The name of her firstborn, Reuben, meant "to see." Maybe the question Leah was trying to ask Jacob was, "Can you see me?"

So she had a second son whom she named Simeon, meaning "to hear." Perhaps she was asking, "Jacob, if you can't see me, can you at least hear me?"

Again, it was obvious that God was hearing her, but Jacob wasn't. Why didn't Jacob hear her? Because he wasn't listening.

Then Leah had a third son, whom she named Levi, which meant "to feel": "Okay Jacob, since you aren't seeing or hearing me, can you at least feel me?"

Listen to her words in verse 32: "The LORD has noticed my misery, and now my husband will love me."

The worst thing in the world is to be beautiful on the outside, but ugly on the inside. Oh, Rachel had a smooth walk and looks to die for. But the girl with the curves had no character.

She soon realized that Jacob neither saw nor heard her. He didn't even feel her. Let's be honest. We all know the world loves shapely Rachels. She was a perfect ten, a trophy wife, if you will. On the one hand, most men want a Rachel and on the other hand most women want to *be* a Rachel. But the fact is, there are more Leahs than Rachels. And it's better to be a real Leah than a fake Rachel. The worst thing in the world is to be beautiful on the outside, but ugly on the inside. Oh, Rachel had a smooth walk and looks to die for. But the girl with the curves had no character.

You will never be the Leah that God created you to be if you're trying to be the Rachel you desire to be. Marilyn Monroe once said that wanting to be someone else was a waste of who you were. For sure there may be someone who is prettier, smarter, taller, darker, thinner, richer, or cuter than you. But they will never be you.

Here's the turning point. Leah had another son, and she named him Judah, which means "praise."

What were you trying to say, Leah? Maybe something like this:

Leah realized she would never be beautiful in the eyes of Jacob. She would have to discover her beauty in the eyes of God.

"I've had it with you, Jacob. I'm going to get my mind off you and focus on the Lord. All this time, I've been trying to get your attention and ignoring the attention I was getting from the Lord. Every time you broke my heart, God put it back together again. So I've come down here to praise Him."

Leah realized she would never be beautiful in the eyes of Jacob. She would have to discover her beauty in the eyes of God. She realized it was easier to please the Lord than it was to please people. Leah was not a centerfold, but she had discovered that beauty was a reflection of the interior, not the exterior.

...for man looks at the outward appearance, but the LORD looks at the heart. — 1 Samuel 16:7 (NKJV)

We can live according to our worth or we can live according to our weakness.

Psalm 139:14 tells me I am "fearfully and wonderfully made." Genesis 1:27 tells us we're created in God's image. Maybe we can't look like Rachel. But guess what—we can look like the Lord!

Here's a final truth to ponder in this chapter: "For we are God's handiwork, created in Christ Jesus to do good works, which God prepared in advance for us to do" (Ephesians 2:10, NIV).

WORKBOOK

Chapter Three Questions

Question: Do you place value on yourself? In which areas of your life do you find it easiest to have self-value, and in which areas do you find it most difficult?

_____

_____

_____

_____

_____

_____

_____

_____

_____

_____

_____

_____

_____

_____

_____

Question: In which areas of your life have you experienced low self-esteem? What could you do, or what did you do, to increase your self-esteem?

_____

_____

_____

_____

_____

_____

_____

_____

_____

_____

_____

_____

_____

_____

Question: When have you tried to please others rather than the Lord? When have you tried to please the Lord first? Which was easier?

_____

_____

_____

_____

_____

_____

_____

_____

_____

_____

_____

_____

_____

_____

_____

_____

Summary: If somebody asks, "Where are you going?" tell them, "I'm going out with *me*." Low self-esteem is generally caused by the abuse, the absence, or the apathy of a significant person in your life. When we fail to value ourselves, we live through substitutes. The worst thing in the world is to be beautiful on the outside but ugly on the inside. Oh, Rachel had a smooth walk and looks to die for. But the girl with the curves had no character. We can live according to our worth, or we can live according to our weakness. Maybe we can't look like Rachel. But guess what—we can look like the Lord!

Notes

CHAPTER FOUR

Embracing Your Destiny

Then God said, "Yes, but your wife Sarah will bear you a son, and you will call him Isaac. I will establish my covenant with him as an everlasting covenant for his descendants after him." — **Genesis 17:19 (NIV)**

In Hebrews 11, we find what is sometimes called the Roll Call of Faith. Hebrews 11:8-11 describes how Abraham, by faith—even though he was past age—and Sarah, who was barren, were enabled to become parents because they considered Him faithful who had made the promise. "And so from this one man, and he as good as dead, came descendants as numerous as the stars in the sky and as countless as the sand on the seashore" (Hebrews 11:12, NIV).

You've heard it said that behind every great man is a great woman. This would certainly be true of Abraham and Sarah. Until her death in Genesis 23, Abraham had Sarah's unwavering support at every point in his somewhat peculiar pilgrimage. Even when Abraham sacrificed her to protect himself, Sarah went right along with the plan. 1 Peter 3:6 notes that she obeyed Abraham, even calling him "lord."

Think about Abraham for a moment. God called him to leave everything—his relatives, his region, and his religion—to go to a land God did not immediately disclose. Hebrews 11:8 tells us, "By faith Abraham obeyed..." (ESV). The only thing God provided for Abraham was a promise. In Genesis 12:2-3, God said to him, "I will make you into a great nation, and I will bless you; I will make your name great, and you will be a blessing. I will bless those who bless you, and whoever curses you I will curse; and all peoples on earth will be blessed through you" (NIV).

Every person who has achieved successes, like Abraham, needs to recognize the sacrifices of people like Sarah.

Abraham left for an unknown destination with only a promise. What is interesting is that God made this promise of posterity to a man who was seventy-five years old, a man with no children and a barren wife! Although Abraham's journey would involve one challenge after another, God would bring his promise to pass some twenty-four years later. Isaac, the son of promise, was born to Abraham when he was one hundred years old and Sarah was ninety.

Every person who has achieved successes, like Abraham, needs to recognize the sacrifices of people like Sarah. While Abraham has been called "the father of the faithful," we would never have known anything about the Jewish people had it not been for what God did in the life of Sarah. Her story made Abraham's possible.

God's promise to Abraham could not come to pass until His promise to Sarah came to pass.

Abraham's destiny was revealed in Genesis 12:2-3, when God promised to make him into a great nation and to bless him. But Sarah's destiny was revealed in chapter 17, verse 16, where the Lord tells Abraham, "I will bless her and will surely give you a son by her. I will bless her so that she will be the mother of nations; kings of peoples will come from her" (NIV).

God's promise to Abraham could not come to pass until His promise to Sarah came to pass. While it took years—even generations—for Abrahams's promise to become reality, Sarah's promise was realized in Genesis 21:1-2:

> *Now the LORD was gracious to Sarah as he had said, and the LORD did for Sarah what he had promised. Sarah became pregnant and bore a son to Abraham in his old age, at the very time God had promised him.*

Sarah was eighty-nine when she bore a son to Abraham, who was ninety-nine. And they named him Isaac. Sarah supported the destiny of her husband. Given her circumstances, however, she could not embrace her own destiny. She didn't understand that Abraham's destiny couldn't be realized without her, or that her story made his possible.

When we take matters into our own hands, we take shortcuts that can lead to dead ends. Shortcuts tempt us to take detours, which are never as good as the main road.

God revealed Abraham's destiny in chapter 12, and Sarah's in chapter 17. *Her* destiny would be realized in chapter 21. But it would take generations for *his* destiny to be realized. Don't lose hope because you're behind somebody. It might just be that you're like Sarah, and your story has to come to pass before somebody else's story can be realized.

But we also need to look at the dark side of Sarah's life, because she shows the problems that can arise when we take matters into our own hands. Sarah made the mistake of trying to hurry God, when things weren't moving at the speed she was wanting. But we all need to learn that God is never in a hurry. When we take matters into our own hands, we take shortcuts that can lead to dead ends. Shortcuts tempt us to take detours, which are never as good as the main road.

In chapter 15, Abraham had come to believe God's promise of posterity, but unfortunately Sarah was so preoccupied by what she *couldn't* do that she couldn't understand what God *could* do. Our limits are not God's limits.

It had been ten years since God made that promise to Abraham in chapter 16. But at this point he was getting older and Sarah was still barren. It didn't look as if what God had promised was going to happen. So Sarah proposed to Abraham that he procreate with her Egyptian maidservant, Hagar. And as a result of this arrangement, Ishmael, the son of convenience, was born.

Just because God allows something does not mean He ordains it.

The problem was that although Sarah, Abraham, and Hagar were all fine with this idea, it was not God's plan. Sarah's plan worked for Sarah's purposes, but not for God's purposes. Just because God allows something does not mean He ordains it. The Scottish novelist George McDonald was right when he said that whatever man did without God would either fail miserably or succeed even more miserably.

The whole point of faith is to embrace what God has ordained for our lives even when we cannot see it, feel it, or understand it. Sarah did not believe her story because at that point she did not believe God. In fact, she laughed at the whole idea. It's one thing to believe *in* God, but

something else to believe God! To believe *in* God is a
matter of principle, but to believe God is a matter of
practice.

Why was it so hard for Sarah to believe what God had
promised? Well, old Sarah was well beyond the age of
childbearing. By her own admission, she was worn out.
And her husband was even older and beyond the years of
productivity, without the benefit of a particular
prescription.

*Where is the Sarah of today? Do you know
someone like her? Are you like her?*

In their culture, Sarah's childlessness was a social
disgrace, and she had accepted her plight without respect
to her promise. She was operating according to her past,
rather than her future. She seemed to be consumed with
her own limitations. She may have been listening for
God, but she was evidently not hearing God, because
faith comes by hearing.

Where is the Sarah of today? Do you know someone
like her? Are *you* like her? There are women like Sarah
in apparently hopeless situations who have not yet begun
to operate in their promises.

Does your future look bleak? Are your dreams
overdue? Do your aspirations appear to be barren, your
expectations dashed? Have you been listening for God
without having heard Him? Here's what He has been
telling you:

"I know the plans I have for you," declares the LORD,
*"plans to prosper you and not to harm you, plans to give
you hope and a future."* — **Jeremiah 29:11 (NIV)**

Like Sarah, we may find it hard to believe that great
things could happen to us. It seems impossible that we
could be the head and not the tail, the lender instead of
the borrower. Perhaps we've not yet faced ourselves in
the mirror and said, "I can do all things through Christ
who strengthens me" (Philippians 4:13, NKJV).

*Against all odds, Sarah conceived! At
ninety years old, she gave birth to a son.*

Are we having trouble sleeping at night, or even
eating? Let us be of good cheer, because Jesus has
overcome the world. Not only that, but He will keep in
perfect peace those whose minds are steadfast, because
they trust in Him (Isaiah 26:3, NKJV).

Remember, God has not given us a spirit of timidity,
but a spirit of power, of love, and of self-discipline. We
are not to be anxious about anything, but in everything,
by prayer and petition, with thanksgiving, to present our
requests to God. And the peace of God, which transcends
all understanding, will guard our hearts and our minds in
Christ Jesus (Philippians 4:6-7, NIV).

Remember the words of Genesis 21:1: "Now the
LORD was gracious to Sarah as he had said" (NIV).

Does it feel like the odds are against you? Against all odds, Sarah conceived! At ninety years old, she gave birth to a son. Can't you picture her at the hospital, walking up to the window of the nursery and being asked, "Which one is your great-grand-baby?" Imagine Sarah proudly saying, "It took me ninety years, but that one's mine."

Like Sarah, you might be someone whose story was never supposed to happen. You weren't born with a silver spoon in your mouth. You were from the wrong side of the tracks. You may have emerged from the ashes of a broken, dysfunctional family. A significant person may have left you, but God took care of you.

We need to be careful how we treat our Sarahs, because if her promise hadn't been realized, Abraham's promise wouldn't have been realized either.

They said we wouldn't make it. They said we couldn't take it. They said we'd never amount to anything, *but God.* They wrote us off. We were down for the count, *but God.*

Why is Sarah so significant? Well, none of our stories are ours exclusively. Our story may be the conclusion to somebody else's story. But it's also the *introduction* to somebody else's story.

Whatever accolades were heaped on Abraham would not have been possible had God not done a miracle in the life of Sarah. God promised posterity to Abraham. There could not have been a great nation without Isaac. But there wouldn't have been an Isaac without Sarah.

There's a Sarah in everybody's life. Maybe it's not a spouse, as with Abraham, but our Sarah is that person whose dreams made ours possible. We need to be careful how we treat our Sarahs, because if her promise hadn't been realized, Abraham's promise wouldn't have been realized either.

Maybe we ought to change our prayers from "Lord, this is what I want you to do for me" to "Lord, I'm available to do what you will through me."

Our Sarah is the one who opened doors for us to walk through, even if she never got to walk through them. Our Sarah is the one who paved the roads on which we travel. The foundation of our success was laid on Sarah's blood, sweat, and tears.

What can we learn from her story?

First, Sarah teaches us how to support what God is doing in the life of somebody else. See, whenever we are preoccupied with bringing other folks down, we don't have time to lift up ourselves. We need all of us to make it.

Second, Sarah teaches us that great things can happen to us in the face of our greatest challenges, because God can handle what we can't.

Third, the essence of our faith has more to do with what God wants to do *through* us than with what He can do *for* us. Maybe we ought to change our prayers from "Lord, this is what I want you to do for me" to "Lord, I'm available to do what you will through me."

Fourth, our lives should never be defined by our dilemma, but by our destiny. As with Abraham and Sarah, God will speak His promise into our predicament.

And we know that in all things God works for the good of those who love him, who have been called according to his purpose. — **Romans 8:28 (NIV)**

WORKBOOK

Chapter Four Questions

Question: What does God promise in Genesis 12:2-3? Why are God's promises difficult to believe sometimes?

_____

_____

_____

_____

_____

_____

_____

_____

_____

_____

_____

_____

_____

_____

_____

Question: When have you tried to take matters into your own hands instead of trusting God? How did the situation turn out?

_____

_____

_____

_____

_____

_____

_____

_____

_____

_____

_____

_____

_____

_____

Question: Do you know someone like Sarah (maybe yourself!), who is so anxious about something that he or she struggles to believe God's promises? How can you, or this person, overcome such doubt and anxiety?

_____

_____

_____

_____

_____

_____

_____

_____

_____

_____

_____

_____

_____

_____

_____

_____

Summary: Every person who has achieved successes, like Abraham, needs to recognize the sacrifices of people like Sarah. God's promise to Abraham could not come to pass until His promise to Sarah came to pass. When we take matters into our own hands, we take shortcuts that can lead to dead ends. Shortcuts tempt us to take detours that are never as good as the main road. Just because God allows something does not mean He ordains it. Where is the Sarah of today? Do you know someone like her? Are _you_ like her? Against all odds, Sarah conceived! We need to be careful how we treat our Sarahs, because if her promise hadn't been realized, Abraham's promise wouldn't have been realized, either. Maybe we ought to change our prayers from "Lord, this is what I want You to do for me" to "Lord, I'm available to do what You will through me."

Notes

CHAPTER FIVE

"I Know Why the Caged Bird Sings"

I Know Why the Caged Bird Sings by Maya Angelou is a literary critique of the social dynamics working to the disadvantage of colored people in America, specifically women.

Most of us at various points in our lives have been defeated, disillusioned, or debilitated by some oppressive entity.

In this age of luxury, it is easy to mask our frailty and frustration with the money we have, the people we know, the jobs we work, the clothes we wear, the cars we drive, and the houses we live in. But the truth is, most of us at various points in our lives have been defeated, disillusioned, or debilitated by some oppressive entity.

Aren't there times in our lives when we are but caged birds singing?

Such was the case with Hannah, whose story we read about in the first chapter of 1 Samuel. A man named Elkanah had two wives, Hannah and Peninnah. Peninnah had children but Hannah did not. Annually, Elkanah would go with both of his wives to worship at Shiloh, the place where the Ark of the Covenant was located at that time. But there was tension between Elkanah's two wives as a result of Peninnah's taunting, and it caused Hannah a lot of grief.

One day, Hannah decided to go to the Lord's house to pray about her situation.

"If you will only give me a son," she pleaded with God, "I'll give him to you for his entire life."

Hannah is defeated and depressed in chapter one, but is delighting in her deliverance in chapter two.

Hannah returned home and God heard Hannah's prayers, for soon afterward she became pregnant and gave birth to a son. She named him Samuel, which means "God heard me," and she remembered the promise she had made to the Lord.

Hannah's name appears in only two chapters of the Bible. Hannah is defeated and depressed in chapter 1, but is delighting in her deliverance in chapter 2.

How do you move from misery to worship? How do you get from being defeated to being delivered?

Hannah teaches us a couple of valuable lessons about life. First, she teaches us how to close a bad chapter. 1 Samuel 1:28 tells us that they worshipped God. What a way to finish! And not only does Hannah teach us how to close a bad chapter in life, but she also teaches us how to open a new one.

Whenever it was time to go to church, Peninnah would taunt Hannah about her childlessness.

But there are difficulties in this story, which we discover when we dig a little deeper. 1 Samuel 1:5 tells us that Hannah's husband loved her, but he had another wife, Peninnah, as well. The second issue was that the Lord had closed Hannah's womb, so she carried the social stigma that went along with barrenness.

On top of that, it seemed the other wife—Hannah's rival, if you will—loved to rub it in. Whenever it was time to go to church, Peninnah would taunt Hannah about her childlessness. To add insult to injury, when Hannah did make it to church, her pastor thought she was drunk.

But what appeared to be the problem in this dysfunctional relationship might not have been the real problem. The real problem was that Hannah was a broken woman.

She was broken physically, because we learn from 1 Samuel 1:7 that she was weeping and refusing to eat. Not only was she broken physically, but she was also broken emotionally. Verse 8 tells us she was downhearted. Verse 10 tells us she was also broken spiritually, for her soul was bitter.

Then, according to verses 15 and 16, she was broken mentally. She was "deeply troubled"—if not clinically depressed, then consumed by anguish and grief.

Hannah made the mistake of seeing herself in terms of her physical deficiency. She also made the mistake of internalizing somebody else's problem.

So Hannah was broken. But the social issues she faced were even more complex. Hannah was challenged by the expectations of her day. In the culture in which she lived, a woman's personhood was defined by her relationship with her husband, and the greatest gift a woman could give a man was a son. A barren woman was worthless.

Hannah made the mistake of seeing herself in terms of her physical deficiency. She also made the mistake of internalizing somebody else's problem. The story does not begin with her having a problem with Peninnah. The whole issue is that Peninnah had a problem with Hannah.

Can I say to some Hannahs who might be reading this: Peninnah's problem doesn't have to be your problem! It's one thing for Peninnah to call you something. But it's something else if you respond to it! Peninnah's problem was that she had to put Hannah down in order to feel good about herself. Shame on her!

This is really at the root of all racism, sexism, and classism. Someone has to be negated or depersonalized to authenticate the deficient personhood of another. Hannah had not learned how to love herself. Her outlook on life was defined by her childlessness, because her culture had taught her that children brought fulfillment.

Since she had no children, she did not expect fulfillment either. Until she made the decision to live above the needling of her rival and go to the temple, Hannah was a classic example of self-negation.

The turning point for Hannah was when she reached out to the Lord in her pain.

Let's be clear: we will never be happy trying to live up to the expectations of others. We know people can be fake, people can be fickle, and people can be funny. Sometimes they just wake up grumpy. Some folks will speak to us one week and not the next. And some will love us only while they need us. Thus, we cannot live our lives based on the expectations of others. Nor can we live by their approval, their opinions, or their criticisms.

The turning point for Hannah was once she reached out to the Lord in her pain. Look at what 1 Samuel 1:10 says: "And she was in bitterness of soul, and prayed to the LORD and wept in anguish" (NKJV). Hannah recognized that she could not get what she really needed from another human being. What she could not get from a relationship or a marriage, only God could provide.

"I'm liable to worry myself sick by talking to people who cannot or will not help me," thought Hannah. "So I'm going to get myself together and go to church. I'm going to talk to my God!"

She shifted her gaze from the horizontal to the vertical and poured her heart to her Creator.

"I've no time for poetry," Hannah told Him. "I need you to hear me. My heart is broken!"

Hannah learned to focus on the real rather than the superficial.

Despite the constraints of her culture, Hannah was finally able to see herself as God saw her. If we're going to learn to live meaningful, purposeful lives, we need to stop looking at ourselves through the eyes of people and see ourselves through the eyes of God. We need to stand before the mirror and say:

"I'm more than lips and hips, and there's more to me than eyes and thighs. I'm wonderfully and fearfully made! I have been made in the image and likeness of God. I'm the crown jewel of His creation. I'm the light of the world. I'm the salt of the earth. I'm a city that sits on a hill. I'm a royal priesthood. I'm a child of God!"

Hannah learned to focus on the real rather than the superficial.

"I wanted a son," she thought, "but I wanted a son so that others would see me differently. I wanted a son so I could measure up to the expectations of others. Well, I still want a son, but this time I want a son for the right reasons. Lord, I want you to give me a son, and once you give him to me, I'm going to give him right back to you."

We find unprecedented fulfillment when we give God all we have. He doesn't just want our praise; He'll handle our problems, too.

The next time they all went to church, Hannah's offering was her son! There are some things God will give us once we decide we can give them back to Him.

In chapter two, Hannah was delighting in her deliverance.

"God's in a class all by himself," she was saying. "God can turn the tide. And when God turns the tide, the mighty fall and the weak are victorious. When God turns the tide, the rich go hungry and the poor get fed. When God turns the tide, the fruitful grieve and the barren produce."

Why should I feel discouraged,
Why should the shadows come,
Why should my heart be lonely
And long for Heav'n and home,
When Jesus is my portion?
My constant friend is He:
His eye is on the sparrow,

And I know He watches me;
His eye is on the sparrow,
And I know He watches me.

"Let not your heart be troubled,"
His tender word I hear,
And resting on His goodness,
I lose my doubts and fears;
Tho' by the path He leadeth
But one step I may see:
His eye is on the sparrow,
And I know he watches me;
His eye is on the sparrow,
And I know he watches me.

Whenever I am tempted,
Whenever clouds arise,
When songs give place to sighing,
When hope within me dies,
I draw the closer to Him,
from care He sets me free;
His eye is on the sparrow,
And I know he watches me;
His eye is on the sparrow,
And I know he watches me.[3]
— Civilla D. Martin, 1866-1948

WORKBOOK

Chapter Five Questions

Question: When in your life have you felt like a caged bird singing?

_____

_____

_____

_____

_____

_____

_____

_____

_____

_____

_____

_____

_____

_____

Question: How do you move from misery to worship?
How do you get from being defeated to being delivered?

_____

_____

_____

_____

_____

_____

_____

_____

_____

_____

_____

_____

_____

Question: Have you ever tried to live up to other
people's expectations? Did you ever live up to those
expectations, or did you always come up short?

_____

_____

_____

_____

_____

_____

_____

_____

_____

_____

_____

_____

_____

_____

_____

Summary: Most of us at various points in our lives have been debilitated by some oppressive entity. Hannah is defeated and depressed in chapter one, but is delighting in her deliverance in chapter two. Peninnah would often taunt Hannah about her childlessness, and Hannah made the mistake of seeing herself in terms of her physical deficiency. The turning point for Hannah was when she reached out to the Lord in her pain. Like Hannah, we must learn God's purpose for our lives.

Notes

_____

_____

_____

_____

_____

_____

_____

_____

_____

_____

_____

_____

_____

_____

_____

_____

_____

_____

_____

_____

_____

_____

CHAPTER SIX

What About Us?

The one and only James Brown, the Godfather of Soul, said it best in "It's a Man's Man's World": "This is a man's world but it wouldn't be nothing ... without a woman or a girl." If you've ever thought you couldn't get along with a woman, try getting along without one.

Sexism has to be as painful and disparaging as racism or classism. Its implicit disdain and lack of appreciation for persons on the grounds of gender often perpetuates the devaluation, dehumanization, and depersonalization of women.

There is a unique story found in Numbers 27. It's about the single daughters of Zelophehad. Their father had died and they had no brothers, and these sisters approached Moses with a question.

"Why should our father's name disappear from his clan because he had no son?" they demanded. "Give us property among our father's relatives." In other words, "What about us?"

Moses brought their case before the Lord, and was told, "What Zelophehad's daughters are saying is right. You must certainly give them property as an inheritance among their father's relatives, and turn their father's inheritance over to them."

While the African-American church has historically been vocal about racism and even classism, it is noticeably silent on issues of sexism. Our silence may unintentionally imply our consent. Though we might turn deaf ears and cover our eyes, it is impossible to ignore the chauvinistic principles and practices that are oppressive to women.

These single women—who have no father and no brothers—are insisting on getting what they feel is their due, despite not having a man in their lives.

It's not a new ideology. We must be honest about the patriarchal prejudices found even in the pages of Holy Writ, since the scriptures arise out of the social order of a male-dominant society. But the convictions of the Bible are not contingent upon the culture of its context.

The story in our text emphatically bears witness to this. These single women—who have no father and no brothers—are insisting on getting what they feel is their due, despite not having a man in their lives.

What a story! What courage! What audacity! They stand up for themselves and respectfully ask for what they would have had coming to them if only they had been men. This story helps us to understand the heart of God, who values and validates persons without respect to gender, culture, or any other circumstance beyond human control.

Let's talk first about what the culture dictated, for it would be irresponsible to deny the reality of the patriarchal mind-set that governed the ancient world. Such a perspective permeates life even today.

Throughout the course of human history, women have been treated as property and been seen as inferior. In many respects, they have been relegated to the status of second-class citizens.

In early biblical times, a father's property was divided among his sons. The oldest son received a birthright that entitled him to a double portion of his father's wealth. Upon the death of the father, the eldest son became the head of the family and was responsible to care for his widowed mother and any unwed sisters.

Their father was no longer responsible for them and they received no inheritance of land or property from his death.

When the daughters or sisters got married, they became fully fledged members of their husband's family. Their father was no longer responsible for them and they received no inheritance of land or property from his death.

*How do women maximize their promise and
potential in a male dominant society?*

But the problem in this passage was that these sisters had no men in their lives—no father to embrace them, no brothers to fight their battles, and no husbands to love them. Perhaps they didn't even have friends to provide "sensual" benefits. Since there was no statutory provision for their wellbeing, they were between a rock and a hard place!

The question is, how do women maximize their promise and potential in a male-dominant society?

The daughters of Zelophehad were challenging a culture that denied them what they would have received if only they had been male. They recognized that the law only considered the interests of men. But they were adamant about receiving what God had promised. They knew they didn't have a leg to stand on—in that culture—but they were unwavering.

There are some remarkable lessons in this story that might bring encouragement to women who are single. The fact is, this story would never have seen the light of day if these women had had brothers or husbands.

The point is, they found favor in the heart of God before they could find love in the hearts of men. In her book *The Sam Syndrome*, Deborah Dunn said that some women derive their value from men and see their purpose in life as finding true love.[4]

She said these kind of women feel as if something is wrong with them if a man does not love them. Often they overlook good men because they might not be sexy or rich, and they sabotage good relationships for no apparent reason. They walk over good men to get to no-good men. Some are often drawn to emotionally unstable men, feeling the need to rescue them.

Being a man is more than just having a different reproductive anatomy. Men are called to be protectors, providers, and priests for their families. Yet, amazingly, there are men who can get a woman but can't get a job. And there are people, particularly women, who feel that having somebody is better than having nobody.

The daughters of Zelophehad obviously understood that they had worth apart from their circumstances.

At some point in our lives, we must realize we need a partner more than we need a playmate. There comes a time to leave the game on the field and realize that tricks are for kids. Moreover, not everybody who is legal is legitimate!

What a tragedy it would be if our thinking at forty were the same as our thinking at fourteen. The daughters of Zelophehad obviously understood that they had worth apart from their circumstances. They lacked a father, brothers, and husbands, but they had the promises of God. They were not agonizing over who was not in their lives. Their vision of God was not obstructed by who they felt was missing or what they did not have. They knew what they deserved, even without men in their lives.

The daughters of Zelophehad brought their case before Moses, who relayed their request to the Lord. Against the grain of the culture and the laws of the land, God showed favor to these sisters. He said to Moses, according to Numbers 27:7, "What Zelophehad's daughters are saying is right. You must certainly give them property ... and give their father's inheritance to them" (NIV)—although these women had no men in their lives.

Our problem today, as perhaps it was even then, is that we love women but we don't value them.

There is a grammatical anomaly in Numbers 27:7 that speaks to the issue of gender equality. In English, the pronouns *them* and *their* are gender neutral. In the original Hebrew, however, the pronouns *them* and *their* are gender specific. These pronouns are used to replace the personal nouns previously specified. In verse 7, the pronouns employed for *them* and *their* are in the masculine gender, although it is women who are being referred to.

What does this mean for us? Men, treat your daughters with the same dignity as you would treat your sons. Our problem today, as perhaps it was even then, is that we love women but we don't *value* them.

Our assessment of their significance seems to be limited to subjective standards versus objective worth. We place a premium on the external at the expense of the internal. We look for curves rather than character. We fail to recognize that what she has *in* is more important than what she has *on*, and most of us never look beyond lips and hips. I tell you, we should take the time to look at them from the front and not always from behind.

Women should not be merely objects of sexual exploitation. We must recognize and respect their gender-specific roles as God ordained them.

We should learn to touch a woman's heart, her mind, and her soul before we try to touch her body. Women should not be merely objects of sexual exploitation. We must recognize and respect their gender-specific roles as God ordained them.

Men and women are not equal in function, but we are equal in essence. In 1 Corinthians 11:3, Paul says, "But I want you to realize that the head of every man is Christ, and the head of the woman is man, and the head of Christ is God" (NIV).

In Genesis 1:27, we read, "So God created man in His own image; in the image of God He created him; male and female He created them" (NKJV).

Genesis 2:22 explains, "Then the LORD God made a woman from the rib he had taken out of the man, and he brought her to the man" (NIV).

1 Peter 3:7 instructs, "Husbands, in the same way be considerate as you live with your wives, and treat them with respect as the weaker partner..." (NIV).

Not only should men learn how to treat women, but women must learn how to treat themselves.

This does not mean the woman God gave you is inferior. The words in the Greek mean treat her like porcelain, not like an iron pot. You are heirs together in the gracious gift of life. Peter goes on to say that you must do this so that nothing will hinder your prayers.

Not only should men learn how to treat women, but women must learn how to treat themselves. Like the daughters of Zelophehad, many women may have to live without a man in their lives. So how do you get to enjoy life if you have to enjoy it all by yourself?

1. Turn your focus to the vertical rather than the horizontal. Stop thinking about who is not there and enjoy the One who is. Psalm 37:4 says, "Delight yourself in the LORD"—not in a man—"and he will give you the desires of your heart" (ESV).

2. You must understand your own value. There's nothing wrong with you. Find yourself. Be yourself. Get comfortable in the skin you're in. You don't have to compete, you don't have to compare, and you definitely don't have to compromise. Respect yourself at all times, and insist that anybody who wants to deal with you must respect you.

3. You've got to learn how to live from the inside out. Because when you've got what you need on the inside, you won't be tripping over what you lack on the outside.

If you've got a bad attitude, Mary Kay can't fix it.

The Apostle Peter says in 1 Peter 3:3-4, "Your beauty should not come from outward adornment, such as elaborate hairstyles and the wearing of gold jewelry or fine clothes. Rather, it should be that of your inner self, the unfading beauty of a gentle and quiet spirit, which is of great worth in God's sight" (NIV).

If you've got a bad attitude, Mary Kay can't fix it.

WORKBOOK

Chapter Six Questions

Question: How do women maximize their promise and potential in a male-dominant society? What cultural idea did the daughters of Zelophehad challenge?

_____

_____

_____

_____

_____

_____

_____

_____

_____

_____

_____

_____

_____

_____

_____

Question: How can we today treat women with value and dignity? How can women ensure that they themselves are treated with dignity?

_____

_____

_____

_____

_____

_____

_____

_____

_____

_____

_____

_____

_____

_____

Question: What are three ways you can truly enjoy life if you have to enjoy it all by yourself?

_____

_____

_____

Summary: These single women—who had no father and no brothers—insisted on getting what they felt was their due, despite not having a man in their lives. Their father was no longer responsible for them, and they received no inheritance of land or property from his death. The daughters of Zelophehad obviously understood they had worth apart from their circumstances. Our problem today, as perhaps it was even then, is that we love women but we don't *value* them. Women should not be mere objects of sexual exploitation. We must recognize and respect their gender-specific roles as God ordained them. Not only should men learn how to treat women, but also women must learn how to treat themselves.

Notes

CHAPTER SEVEN

Worship at Its Best

What can a sinner teach us about worship? In Luke 7 we read the story of how the Lord Jesus Christ was invited to dinner in the home of Simon, who was a Pharisee. While there, he was approached by a woman who had an immoral lifestyle.

Simon abdicated the customary responsibilities of hospitality in ancient Jewish culture. But this sinful woman went above and beyond traditional practices as she honored Christ. Her unusual actions challenge us to rethink the nature and quality of our worship.

Let's look at these two people—Simon, the Pharisee, and this woman, a sinner. Simon was an example of what worship should *not* be. He was a Pharisee, a group of religious leaders who were the keepers of the traditions of the elders. So he would have been aware of the proper etiquette for entertaining guests in his home.

Upon entering, guests would normally have had their feet washed by a servant, or even by the host himself. At the very least, water would have been provided for the guests to wash their own feet. Guests were also greeted formally with a kiss on the cheek. The host would also anoint the head of the special guest with oil.

Failure to at least offer Jesus water to wash His feet with was not just careless hospitality: It was civil disrespect.

Unfortunately, Simon invited Jesus to dine in his house only to insult him. He did not provide water for the cleansing of Jesus's feet, nor did he greet Him with a kiss or anoint His head with oil. Failure to at least offer Jesus water to wash His feet with was not just careless hospitality: It was civil disrespect.

The real issue may have been deeper than just decorum or protocol. In some ancient traditions, when a superior entered the house of an inferior, the latter washed his feet. The neglect of basic courtesy on the part of Simon may suggest that he had an exalted view of himself and a deficient view of Jesus Christ.

Did he see himself as equal to Christ? Did he view Christ as inferior? The question for us is, what do our own attitudes and actions say about the way we see Christ? How do they relate to our paradigm of worship and ministry?

While Simon was remiss in his hospitality, he was quite critical of the actions of the sinful woman. This woman washed Jesus's feet with her tears, wiped them with her hair, and anointed his feet with perfume. Simon went as far as to raise questions about the character of Jesus.

"If this man were a prophet," he muttered to himself, "he would know who is touching him and what kind of woman she is—that she is a sinner." (Luke 7:39, NIV).

It is not clear what Simon's motives were in inviting Jesus into his house. But clearly it was not to honor Him!

Simon's actions and attitude illustrate some critical dynamics of worship. Here we can learn what worship was never intended to be. It is not clear what Simon's motives were in inviting Jesus into his house. But clearly it was not to honor Him!

The truth is, any activity that does not honor the Lord cannot be called worship. Worship is not an opportunity for self-exaltation, or for advancing our own agendas under the guise of spirituality. It should never be about religious self-indulgence. God is insulted when anything or anybody replaces Him as the object of worship. He is dishonored when we treat Him casually, or when we lose our sense of awe in His presence. We might feel good. We might get happy, jump up high, and shout out loud. But it is never worship when God is disappointed.

Sometimes we are hypercritical in our evaluation of worship. When we look at what others have done or not done, we may leave saying, "They didn't do anything for me today." The reality is, if we ever leave worship complaining, we have nobody to blame but ourselves. Doesn't the Bible say, "Let the redeemed of the LORD say so" (Psalm 107:2, ESV)? It also says, "Let everything that has breath praise the LORD" (Psalm 150:6, ESV).

We often talk about what we expect in worship. But our goal should always be to meet God's expectations.

The fact that Jesus calls Simon's negligence to his attention shows that he came with expectations. We often talk about what *we* expect in worship. But our goal should always be to meet *God's* expectations. If anybody has to be disappointed with what happens in church, let's be sure it isn't God. Simon illustrates everything that worship was never designed to be, while the woman in our story is an example of what really ought to happen when we come to church.

She could not have been any more different from the Pharisee. In fact, she was referred to as "a sinful woman." From all indications, she was a lady of the night. The New Living Translation calls her "immoral," so it seems she had a reputation. Nonetheless, the darkness of her past sins had been overcome by the mercy and forgiveness of Jesus Christ.

As a woman, she would never have been invited to dine in a banquet setting. But wealthy people entertained in their courtyards. These were open for persons to come in and observe the feasts and to listen to the conversations of the important people. This explains how this immoral woman had gained access to Jesus.

Simon was aware of the protocol, but ignored it. This woman knew nothing of the customary etiquette, but won the heart of Christ. What she did went against the grain and violated the ceremonial law, but she pleased the Lord. She knew no protocol. She wasn't even on the program, but at this feast she managed to honor Christ in a manner like no other.

In the ancient culture, hair was indicative of a woman's dignity.

She approached Jesus, weeping. Perhaps these were tears of repentance, or regret, or joy. I like to think they were tears of elation. But these very tears fell on the feet of Jesus and she bowed to the ground in humility and wiped His feet with her hair. This woman took worship to a whole new level.

In the ancient culture, hair was indicative of a woman's dignity, and there she was on her knees, putting her dignity at Jesus' feet. When we come to the feet of Jesus, we ought to forget about what car we drive. When we come to the feet of Jesus, our master's degree ought to not matter. When we come to the feet of Jesus, we ought to put our dignity at his feet. After all, worship isn't about who we are: It's about who *He* is.

Rather than giving the customary kiss on the cheek, the woman kissed His feet. Now, this may not have been "denominationally correct." It wasn't even Jewish! But she seemed to be saying, "I'm not trying to be churchy right now. I'm not trying to be Baptist, Methodist, Jewish, Pentecostal, or Presbyterian. I'm just trying to meet Jesus."

Her worship was costly. But is it really worship if it doesn't cost us anything?

People are sick and tired of pastors fussing about theological differences. They're sick and tired of us arguing about asinine dynamics of our faith when the reality is that people want to see Jesus.

This woman went where nobody else was going. She kissed His feet as a sign of respect, submission, and affection. I don't know why she hung out at His feet. But I believe when she looked at all He was and looked at all she was, she was glad just to be in His presence.

The tradition was to anoint the head. Maybe this woman felt unworthy to anoint His head. But it's clear to me that she had no other agenda than to honor Christ. Her worship was costly. But is it really worship if it doesn't cost us anything?

Simon was watching her. Whatever could have been said about her had already been said, and in any case, folks in that profession usually don't care what anybody says about them. But this woman had her eyes on Jesus.

At this point, Jesus raised a reality check. Simon was negligent in his hospitality but he was critical of this woman and her act of worship. It's amazing how this religious man found it so easy to assess this woman's spiritual condition, but was so blind to his own. He showed her up as a sinner, but didn't realize he was one too.

Christ paid a debt He did not owe because we owed a debt we could not pay.

So Jesus shared a parable with him. He talked about two debtors, one who owed five hundred pieces of silver and one who owed fifty. In neither case could the debtor pay what he owed. So the creditor canceled both debts. That's just what happened at Calvary. Christ paid a debt He did not owe because we owed a debt we could not pay.

Jesus asked him, "Simon, who had the bigger debt?"

"Certainly the one who owed the most," Simon replied.

The parable was pointing to sin on the part of both individuals. But the woman knew she was a sinner, while Simon didn't know he was one.

Meanwhile, this woman wouldn't stop kissing Jesus's feet, and she was probably getting on Simon's nerves. He was wondering why she wouldn't sit down. But you see, all this was brand new to her. She was not a church regular, but was totally consumed by the glory of God.

She didn't know which door to come in, when to sit, when to stand, when to shout, when to run, or when to jump. She only wanted to be in the presence of Jesus Christ. Her worship had not been polluted by the religious status quo. She didn't know any better than to give the Lord the best she had.

She had finally met a man who wasn't looking for lips and hips, someone who could see her from the inside out.

She had just been delivered from her sin, and all she knew was what the Lord had done in her life. Every time she tried to sit down, she thought of something else the Lord had done for her and she got up and kissed His feet again. She had finally met a man who could love her, not just use her. She couldn't sit down because she had finally met a man who wanted to hang out with her longer than thirty minutes. She had finally met a man who wasn't looking for lips and hips, someone who could see her from the inside out. She'd finally heard a man who said, "I love you," and meant it.

WORKBOOK

Chapter Seven Questions

Question: What kind of etiquette do you have toward guests who come into your home?

_____

_____

_____

_____

_____

_____

_____

_____

_____

_____

_____

_____

_____

_____

_____

Question: What do your own attitudes and actions say about the way you see Christ? What are your expectations of God, worship, and ministry?

_____

_____

_____

_____

_____

_____

_____

_____

_____

_____

_____

_____

Question: How do you worship? How do you think you could better meet God's expectations?

_____

_____

_____

_____

_____

_____

_____

_____

_____

_____

_____

_____

_____

_____

_____

_____

_____

Summary: Unfortunately, Simon invited Jesus to dine in his house only to insult Him. Failure to at least offer Jesus water with which to wash His feet was not just careless hospitality. It was civil disrespect. It is not clear what Simon's motives were in inviting Jesus into his house. But clearly it was not to honor Him! The fact that Jesus calls Simon's negligence to his attention shows that He came with expectations. We often talk about what _we_ expect in worship. But our goal should always be to meet _God's_ expectations. In the ancient culture, hair was indicative of a woman's dignity, and there the woman was on her knees, putting her dignity at Jesus's feet. Her worship was costly. Is it really worship if it doesn't cost us anything? Christ paid a debt He did not owe because we owed a debt we could not pay.

Notes

CHAPTER EIGHT

From Misery to Ministry

With every privilege comes problems, and with every problem comes privileges. The truth is, if we removed some of our problems, we would lose all the privileges that accompany them. But we usually become wiser and stronger as a result of some of the things we've gone through.

In Luke 4:38-39, we read: "Now He arose from the synagogue and entered Simon's house. But Simon's wife's mother was sick with a high fever, and they made request of Him concerning her. So He stood over her and rebuked the fever, and it left her. And immediately she arose and served them" (NKJV).

This is a journey from misery to ministry. God has placed several callings on each of us. The first and most significant is the call to *salvation*. Jesus says in Matthew 9:13, "For I did not come to call the righteous, but sinners, to repentance" (NKJV).

Then there is a call to *sanctification*. The Scripture says, "Be holy, because I am holy" (1 Peter 1:16, NIV).

And then there is a call to *service*. Jesus said to His disciples who were fishing, "Follow Me, and I will make you fishers of men" (Matthew 4:19, NKJV). James further admonishes us to be doers of the Word and not merely hearers (James 1:22).

God's will for the believer is neither a life of hedonism (all pleasure) nor a life of hurt (all pain).

Somewhere in the middle of the privilege/pain continuum is the believer's purpose. To live at either extreme is detrimental to us. God's will for the believer is neither a life of hedonism (all pleasure) nor a life of hurt (all pain).

A life of purpose, however, comes with both gloom and glory. Wouldn't it be nice if we always had everything we needed and wanted? Wouldn't it be wonderful if we were always happy? If people always minded their own business? If we were never sick, never broke, never hurt, never angry, never hateful? But unfortunately, earth is not heaven, and "into each life some rain must fall."

Andrae Crouch said it best:

I thank God for the mountains, and I thank Him for the valleys.

I thank Him for the storms He brought me through.

For if I'd never had a problem, I wouldn't know God could solve them,

I'd never know what faith in God could do.

"Through it all," Crouch sang, "I've learned to trust in Jesus."[5]

Many of us have so much more to offer the Kingdom, but because we are wrestling with our own pain, we never live up to the potential God has invested in us.

Countless folks are miserable. Maybe you're not, but you know somebody who is. And until their pain is eradicated, they will never maximize their ministry, their potential, or their possibility.

Peter's mother-in-law is a portrait of both misery and ministry. She portrays the movement from sickness to service, from disease to duty.

The truth is, many of us have so much more to offer the Kingdom, but because we are wrestling with our own pain, we never live up to the potential God has invested in us; nor do we experience lives that are driven by God's purpose and design.

This story portrays misery at its worst. This woman had a fever, which could have been from malaria. It was her fever that prevented her from functioning. In Greek, the word for fever, *pyro*, is the same as the word for fire. She was burning from an intense fire within.

I asked my doctor to explain a fever to me. He told me that it's our body's defense mechanism kicking in. Bacteria can't survive beyond a certain temperature, so when bacteria invades, our body raises its temperature to kill it off.

God might be putting us through the heat and the flames of life to kill off some stuff that is detrimental to our health.

There is a moral here. God might be putting us through the heat and the flames of life to kill off some stuff that is detrimental to our health.

Then my doctor explained that the same fever that was designed to help us could wind up hurting us. (Isn't it interesting how some of the people or things we thought would help us wind up hurting us?)

The woman in our story has a major fever. One of the wonderful things about Luke, who was a physician as well as a writer, was his attention to detail. He caught stuff that Matthew and Mark just slip over. Luke says Peter's mother-in-law was in the grip of a burning fever. So the issue was not that she had a fever. The issue was that the fever had her!

And the cure was beyond Luke's medical capacity. Only Jesus could deal with her sickness. Let me ask you. What "has" you? We need to be careful about two things—the things we won't let go of, and the things that won't let go of us. When there are things we won't let go of, we call them sins of affection, but when there are things that won't let us go, we call them addictions. Maybe we think of addictions as drugs or alcohol. But we can also be addicted to chocolate cake. That's when we may get into trouble.

When a fever is minor, it's a symptom. But when it's a *great* fever, it's a problem. A lot of folks can't distinguish between symptoms and problems. Things we think of as mere symptoms could very well be problems.

I suggest we all have three options as to how we're going to live our lives:

1. The pleasure-driven life
2. The pain-driven life
3. The purpose-driven life

Those who live the pleasure-driven life have a simple creed: eat, drink, and be merry, one club after another, one vacation after another, one party after another. Those who are pleasure-driven have reduced life to whatever looks, tastes, smells, and feels good. For them it's all play and no work, like the man who's thirty years old with a Playstation and no job.

Then there's the pain-driven life. Some people are obsessed with the pathology of discomfort. They always have to have a problem and they never have a good day.

Someone might say, "The sun is shining."

And the pain-driven person might reply: "Yeah, but they say it's a twenty percent chance of rain."

Let's enjoy the eighty percent chance of sunshine!

Pain-driven people are defined by their issues. That's all they talk about. When our issues define us, we are debilitated and ultimately defeated by them. Pain-driven people might say, "If the Lord releases me from pain, He might expect something from me."

People who live purpose-driven lives find joy and contentment in service.

Charlie Brown was having a bad day and Lucy said, "Charlie, I hope you feel better." Charlie replied, "Lucy, I don't *want* to feel better."[6]

There's the pain-driven life and the pleasure-driven life, and thirdly the purpose-driven life. People who live purpose-driven lives find joy and contentment in service. They live for three objectives—their own growth, the good of others, and the glory of God.

As believers, we ought to be growing. And we ought to be preoccupied—not with our own good, but with the good of other people. Ultimately this is not for our glory, but for the glory of God.

In this text, we see misery at its worst, but also ministry at its best. Look at Jesus's ministry to the woman. We know she's got a great fever and the fever has a grip on her.

Matthew puts this miracle in the context of several other miracles that deal with people who are socially outcast. Jesus heals a leper—by placing His hands on him. Then He speaks a word and heals the servant of a gentile centurion. Then there is this woman.

*One reason we can't get anywhere with
some of the people we love is that we try to
speak to them when we really ought to be
speaking to their problem.*

Matthew tells us He touched her and the fever left
her. At first glance, we may see nothing unusual in that.
But if we look at the incident against the backdrop of
first-century eastern (and Jewish) culture, we spot two
things that are problematic.

First, a rabbi never touched a woman who was not his
wife. Second, to touch a woman or a person with fever
was against the law.

When it came to miracles, Jesus went against
protocol. Matthew says He touched her and the fever left
her. Mark and Matthew imply that she was bedridden
and burning with fever. Mark notes that not only did He
touch her, but He also raised her up and then the fever
left.

But in his account, Doctor Luke mentions two other
details that only a physician would have noted. He says
Jesus *stood over* her. He positioned Himself in the place
of authority. And when He did so, everything under Him
was subject to His power. When Jesus takes authority in
our life, it doesn't matter what our problem is.

The next thing Jesus did was to rebuke the fever. He
didn't say anything to the woman, but rather He spoke
straight to her problem. One reason we can't get
anywhere with some of the people we love is that we try

to speak to them when we really ought to be speaking to their problem.

Has God done anything in your life? What have you done for Him?

We've talked about Jesus's ministry to the woman. Now let's look at her ministry to Him. You know what I like about this woman? Nowhere in Scripture is there a record of what she said. She doesn't talk. She acts. She doesn't have anything to say, but look at what happened after Jesus healed her. This helps us understand what comes after deliverance. The Message says, "Before they knew it, she was up getting dinner for them" (Luke 4:38-39)!

Has God done anything in your life? What have you done for Him? Maybe, like this woman, you recognize it's time to get beyond your pain, or even your pleasure, and start walking in your purpose. Today is your day!

WORKBOOK

Chapter Eight Questions

Question: Has God put you through heat and flames in life to kill off stuff that is detrimental to your health? Is your life much better now that you don't have those things in your life?

_____

_____

_____

_____

_____

_____

_____

_____

_____

_____

_____

_____

_____

_____

Question: Which element—plain, pleasure, or purpose—
is currently driving your life? What do you perceive to
be God's purpose for your life?

_____

_____

_____

_____

_____

_____

_____

_____

_____

_____

_____

_____

Question: What has God done in your life? What have
you done for Him?

_____

_____

_____

_____

_____

_____

_____

_____

_____

_____

_____

_____

_____

_____

_____

Summary: God's will for the believer is neither a life of hedonism (all pleasure) nor a life of hurt (all pain). Many of us have so much more to offer the Kingdom, but because we are wrestling with our own pain, we never live up to the potential God has invested in us; nor do we experience lives that are driven by God's purpose and design. God might be putting us through the heat and the flames of life to kill off some stuff that is detrimental to our health. People who live purpose-driven lives find joy and contentment in service. They live for three objectives—their own growth, the good of others, and the glory of God. When they minister, they don't just talk to people—they speak straight to their problems.

Notes

CHAPTER NINE

The Life You Have Always Wanted

In John chapter 4, we read how Jesus was walking through Samaria, and He came to a town called Sychar, near the plot of ground Jacob had given to his son Joseph.

Jacob's well was there, and Jesus, tired from the journey, sat down by the well. It was about noon. Here he encountered the Samaritan woman:

> *A woman from Samaria came to draw water. Jesus said to her, "Give Me a drink." (For his disciples had gone away into the city to buy food.) The Samaritan woman said to Him, "How is it that you, a Jew, ask for a drink from me, a woman of Samaria?" (For Jews have no dealings with Samaritans.) Jesus answered her, "If you knew the gift of God, and who it is that is saying to you, 'Give me a drink,' you would have asked him, and he would have given you living water." The woman said to him, "Sir, You have nothing to draw water with, and the well is deep. Where do you get that living water? Are you greater than our father Jacob? He gave us the well and drank from it himself, as*

did his sons and his livestock." Jesus said to her, "Everyone who drinks of this water will be thirsty again, but whoever drinks of the water that I will give him will never be thirsty again. The water that I will give him will become in him a spring of water welling up to eternal life."
— ***John 4:7-14 (ESV)***

Then Jesus came along and offered this woman the life she—as well as we—always wanted.

It is Jesus Christ Himself who offers the better promise. He says, "In this world you will have trouble. But take heart! I have overcome the world" (John 16:33, NIV).

Most of us know already that an assurance of endless bliss is the stuff of fairytales. We can relate better to the maternal testimony in the second line of Langston Hughes's poem "Mother to Son," which says "Life for me ain't been no crystal stair."

There is much we can learn by reading between the lines of Jesus's conversation with the Samaritan woman. We see in this person's life a seemingly endless cycle of futility and frustration. Then Jesus came along and offered this woman the life she—as well as we—always wanted.

First, let's look at the life we think we want—the life of *comfort*. Most of us long for the American dream: a good education, a promising career, a beautiful home with a white picket fence, a nice ride, a happy marriage with a handsome husband or a pretty wife, a healthy family, a couple of obedient children, four goldfish, three meowing cats, two barking dogs, and perhaps a partridge in a pear tree!

No little girl aspires to a broken heart. We all want, like Cinderella, to be able to say, "...and we lived happily ever after."

We'd all love to be financially solvent, spiritually complete, physically fit, and socially accepted. Oh, how nice it would be to have a mansion on every lot, a Bentley on every block, a yacht at every dock, and a chicken in every pot.

That's the life of *convenience*.

Near the end of this story, we learn a couple of fascinating things about the Samaritan woman. First, she has been married five times. We'd all agree this probably wasn't her childhood dream. No little girl aspires to a broken heart. We all want, like Cinderella, to be able to say, "...and we lived happily ever after."

But where this woman was presently was not her original destination. For as many as five times, she had kissed a prince who had turned out to be a frog. For many people, it's been one relationship after another—one man after another, one woman after another, one job or career or residence after another. For some, it's even been one church after another. The Samaritan woman was not alone in her longing for *commitment*.

The Samaritan woman longed for commitment, but settled for convenience.

When we were children, we were in a hurry to grow up, but we have discovered that adulthood is not what it's cracked up to be. Yes, it's been one disappointment after another, and it's always easier to lose our innocence than to lose our guilt. The life we've come to know has been one thing after another. We never expected to wind up with true enemies, fake friends, and deferred dreams.

In the vernacular of Brother Tyrone Davis, a preacher's son, "If I had the chance to start all over, I'd be wishing today for a four-leaf clover." If only we could turn back the hands of time. If only we knew then what we know now.

We know the Samaritan woman had been married five times. We also know she was involved with a sixth man who Jesus said emphatically was not hers. Whoever he was, it seems he was just not available. He was there, but not there. Maybe his body was with her, but his heart was someplace else.

The Samaritan woman longed for commitment, but settled for convenience. Like many women today, she would rather have a piece of a man than no man at all. But a piece of a man can only offer you a piece of relationship. And a piece of relationship turns into a piece of marriage. And a piece of marriage will give you a piece of family. Your man might be available physically, but perhaps not mentally or emotionally.

To move a relationship to another level requires learning how to love a person from the inside out.

When you get to be a certain age, you want everything in one place. Thank God for growth and maturity. Where I am now, I need you to touch my heart, my mind, and my soul before you touch my body.

If you're trying to move a relationship to another level, you need to learn how to love from the inside out. Because if you're trying to love from the outside in, please know that it won't be long before the external things change.

But when you love her from the inside out, you'll still love her when her teeth are in the jar and her hair is on the dresser. When you love her from the inside out, she doesn't have to be a perfect size six.

So the woman in our text had no marriage, just benefits. She was a girlfriend operating in wife mode, having the role without the ring. And she was stuck in a ceaseless cycle of futility.

Sadly, we all know people who seem to be satisfied with substandard lives of scarcity. They have no dreams, no visions, no goals, no aspirations, no expectations, no ambitions, no aims, no hopes, and no purpose.

*Having everything in life really doesn't
matter if we don't have what really matters.*

The life God is calling us to is one of contentment in
Christ. We must admit that the life we have come to
know may look great, but in many respects we have so
much and yet so little. Sometimes we have more cash
than character, more jewelry than joy, more diamonds
than devotion, and more gold than godliness.

Substance is not always found in success or
significance. Having everything in life really doesn't
matter if we don't have what really matters. Mike
Buchanan says we are trapped in the cult of the next
thing—the next dollar, the next gadget, the next house or
car, the next style, the next man, or the next woman.

Many of us are sick and tired of temporary things. At
this point in my life, I am thanking God for the things
that last forever.

Jesus said in verse 13 that everyone who drank of
worldly water would thirst again. We know this to be
true, because once we ourselves were never satisfied.
Too much was never enough.

But Jesus says that if we drink His water, we will
never thirst again.

WORKBOOK

Chapter Nine Questions

Question: Was your dream always to live the American dream—the life of comfort? Is that how your life has ended up, or were you taken down a different path? Do you have everything you want, or are you still waiting for more?

_____

_____

_____

_____

_____

_____

_____

_____

_____

_____

_____

_____

_____

_____

Question: Being an adult, have you ever wanted to turn back time or start life over? What would you do differently if you had that one chance?

_____

_____

_____

_____

_____

_____

_____

_____

_____

_____

_____

_____

_____

_____

Question: Do you live a satisfied life? Or are you still wanting more out of life? What makes you have a satisfied life, or what drives you to want more?

_____

_____

_____

_____

_____

_____

_____

_____

_____

_____

_____

_____

_____

_____

Summary: It is Jesus Christ Himself who offers the better promise. Jesus came along and offered this woman the life she—as well as we—always wanted. Let's look at the life we think we want: the life of comfort. Most of us long for the American dream. When we were children, we were in a hurry to grow up, but it's been one disappointment after another, and it's always easier to lose our innocence than to lose our guilt. We must admit that the life we have come to know may look great, but in many respects we have so much and yet so little. But the life God is calling us to is one of contentment in Christ. Jesus says if we drink His water, we will never thirst again. Substance is not always found in success or significance.

Notes

_____

_____

_____

_____

_____

_____

_____

_____

_____

_____

_____

_____

_____

_____

_____

_____

_____

_____

_____

_____

_____

_____

CHAPTER TEN

Every Mary Needs an Elizabeth

In this chapter, we will look at two women, each with lives and legacies that are remarkable in their own way. Mary is young; Elizabeth is old. Mary is engaged to Joseph; Elizabeth is married to Zechariah. Mary is a virgin; Elizabeth is barren. We meet them at pivotal, crucial points in God's salvation story.

At that time Mary got ready and hurried to a town in the hill country of Judea, where she entered Zechariah's home and greeted Elizabeth. When Elizabeth heard Mary's greeting, the baby leaped in her womb, and Elizabeth was filled with the Holy Spirit. In a loud voice she exclaimed: "Blessed are you among women, and blessed is the child you will bear! But why am I so favored, that the mother of my Lord should come to me? As soon as the sound of your greeting reached my ears, the baby in my womb leaped for joy. Blessed is she who has believed that the Lord would fulfill his promises to her!" — Luke 1:39-45 (NIV)

The long-awaited, much-anticipated Messiah, the only begotten Son of the Father, Jesus Christ, had been conceived by the Holy Spirit in Mary's virgin womb. And his forerunner, John the Baptist, had been miraculously conceived in Elizabeth's barren womb.

Mary was a young woman who had hopes of beginning a career, finding her prince, getting married, starting a family, and living happily ever after. But God interrupted her plans and called her to His own plans for her life.

What happens in this first chapter of Luke confirms two things: **1)** Every Mary needs an Elizabeth; **2)** Every Elizabeth needs a Mary. Don't we all need the enlightenment, the encouragement, and even the exhortation of seasoned saints? And don't all seasoned saints have the spiritual and moral obligation to impart their wisdom and invest their experiences into the lives of the generations after them?

Mary was a young woman who had hopes of beginning a career, finding her prince, getting married, starting a family, and living happily ever after. But God interrupted her plans and called her to His own plans for her life.

Mary was that girl from the other side of the tracks that nobody noticed. She was overlooked by the masses, but selected by God to bring forth what we all needed.

She had no say in the matter, but surrendered to the will of God for her life.

She had something inside her womb that the man she was pledged to marry did not understand, others did not believe, and she herself could not explain.

Mary was the young lady who put literally everything on the line to please the Lord— her plans, her engagement, her reputation, her body, and ultimately even her life.

Mary was that unlikely person from an unlikely place whom God called for an unlikely purpose. She had no wealth, no influence, no fame, and no fortune. But the angel authenticated the endorsement of God on her life by declaring she was blessed and highly favored. She had no house on the hill, no designer clothing, no rubies or diamonds, dollars or degrees, silver or gold. In fact, all Mary had was what God had placed inside of her.

Mary was the young lady who put literally everything on the line to please the Lord—her plans, her engagement, her reputation, her body, and ultimately even her life. You see, in those days an unwed pregnancy was punishable by death.

There are many Marys, but has anyone seen Elizabeth? The thing is, every Mary needs an Elizabeth, although sometimes it's hard to find one because some sisters have more seniority than spirituality. They might be in your church, but not in the Lord. They might be critical, judgmental, or negative; they might have grown old and mean.

The worst thing that could be said about a woman in that ancient culture was said about Elizabeth.

Sometimes it's hard to find an Elizabeth. Though many are viable candidates for knee and hip replacements, some are still trying to drop it like it's hot. They cannot resist the temptations of their twenties, the thrill of their thirties, or the fun of their forties. They call themselves nifty at fifty, sexy at sixty, sensual at seventy, elegant at eighty, and naughty at ninety. Many who were once foxes are now cougars. In the sixties, they marched with Martin; today, they're dating Jamal.

Yes, sometimes it's hard to find an Elizabeth, but thank God there are still some around.

Elizabeth had a godly character. In fact, both she and her husband Zechariah were upright in the sight of God, observing all the Lord's requirements and regulations blamelessly (Luke 1:6).

Elizabeth was also confident. She teaches us that our significance need not be determined by what the world calls success, and that we can trust God in the face of our shattered dreams.

The worst thing that could be said about a woman in that ancient culture was said about Elizabeth.

But they had no child, because Elizabeth was barren, and they were both well advanced in years. — **Luke 1:7 (NKJV)**

But Elizabeth lived beyond cultural expectations, and she demonstrated holiness in the absence of happiness.

How could Elizabeth have had such confidence in the face of shattered dreams? She didn't have a white picket fence, a split level home, or cars in the driveway. She had no children, but she was able to celebrate God's favor on her life.

Elizabeth reminds us that a dream deferred is not a dream denied. Sister, are you wondering if you can go back to school? Are you wondering if you can finish a degree? Some might not have graduated at eighteen, but they got their GED at twenty-one. They might not have gotten that degree at twenty-two, but they got it at thirty-five, forty-five, or even fifty-five.

A dream deferred is not a dream denied.

You too can make it! Everything you need, God has given to you. A dream deferred is not a dream denied. Look in the mirror every day and tell yourself, "God has not given me a spirit of timidity, but a spirit of power, love, and self-discipline" (2 Timothy 1:7).

You might be forty-five, but you can go back to school. You might've had children earlier than planned, but you can raise them in the nurture and admonition of the Lord. You might not have a man, but you have Jesus. It was He who was there before your man came, and it was He who held you after your man left.

There will always be some people who don't believe in what God is trying to do in your life.

Elizabeth was a woman of character and confidence, and she teaches us how to handle criticism. There will always be those in your life who don't believe. When Mary got pregnant, Joseph decided to put her away quietly. When Elizabeth got pregnant, Zechariah was at church arguing with the angel. Neither Joseph nor Zechariah understood or initially embraced what God was doing in Mary's or Elizabeth's lives.

There will always be some people who don't believe in what God is trying to do in your life. When Mary got pregnant, the angel told her that Elizabeth was pregnant too. Do you know why? Because Elizabeth was the only one with whom Mary could discuss her destiny, because Elizabeth understood destiny.

An eagle somehow wound up in a chicken coop one day. After a while it said to the chickens, "It was good to hang out with you all, but I think I'm kind of wired to mount up on wings and fly."

One of the chickens retorted, "I wouldn't do that if I were you. The last time I tried it, I fell on my behind."

God, deliver us from chicken-minded people! You can't do eagle talk with chickens. They only know how to get to the top of the fence, but eagles know how to get to the mountaintop. You can't discuss destiny with defeated, despondent, or discouraged folks. You can only talk vision and victory with visionary and victorious people. We are called to be eagles! In the words of singer R. Kelly, "I believe I can fly!"

> *But those who hope in the LORD will renew their strength. They will soar on wings like eagles; they will run and not grow weary, they will walk and not faint.* — **Isaiah 40:31 (NIV)**

Elizabeth was positive and affirmative. When Mary came to see her, Elizabeth had an encouraging word. She looked at Mary and said, "Blessed are you among women, and blessed is the child you will bear!" (Luke 1:42, NIV).

"But why me?" Elizabeth must have wondered. "Why am I so favored that the mother of my Lord should come to me?"

She knew something was going on with Mary, because as soon as she heard Mary's voice, the baby in her womb began to leap for joy.

We all need people in our lives who will make us better and wiser and stronger, but too often we only invite people into our lives who will co-sign our foolishness. We need somebody who'll get in our face and tell us when we are wrong. We need somebody who will say, "You know I love you, dear, but I must tell you that you're making a mistake."

Everybody knows Mary, but few know Elizabeth. Yet it's the Elizabeths in life who pave the way for the Marys.

Find yourself an Elizabeth whom you can sit by and glean wisdom from, someone you can call on when things get rough at home, someone whose shoulder you can cry on, someone who has been there, done that. Find someone who will tell you to place your problems in the hands of the Lord.

We meet Mary on other occasions in the Bible. But this is all we hear of Elizabeth. Everybody knows Mary, but few know Elizabeth. Yet it's the Elizabeths in life who pave the way for the Marys.

A young woman might prefer to hang out with other young women, but remember, while a new broom sweeps pretty clean, it's the old broom that knows how to handle the cracks.

If you're a woman with both "seniority" and spirituality, you need to be an Elizabeth. You need to put your arms around a younger woman and love her and nurture her. They don't need your criticism as much as they need your encouragement. Invest in their lives!

Likewise, teach the older women to be reverent in the way they live, not to be slanderers or addicted to much wine ...
— **Titus 2:3 (NIV)**

Every young woman should ask God to reveal her Elizabeth to her. And every seasoned woman should pray to be an Elizabeth. Can you imagine what our churches and communities and families would be like if the Marys and Elizabeths got together?

Chapter Ten Questions

Question: When you were younger, did you have set plan in your head of what you wanted your life to be like? What was that plan? Did God take you down a different course? Have you enjoyed the path that God has taken you down?

_____

_____

_____

_____

_____

_____

_____

_____

_____

_____

_____

_____

_____

_____

_____

Question: What are the characteristics of a Mary? What are the characteristics of an Elizabeth?

_____

_____

_____

_____

_____

_____

_____

_____

_____

_____

_____

_____

_____

_____

Question: Do you have a friend like Elizabeth? Are you yourself more of a Mary or an Elizabeth? What characterstics do you have that define you as more one or the other?

_____

_____

_____

_____

_____

_____

_____

_____

_____

_____

_____

_____

_____

_____

Summary: Don't all seasoned saints have the spiritual and moral obligation to impart their wisdom and invest their experiences into the lives of the generations to follow? Mary was overlooked by the masses, but selected by God to bring forth what we all needed. Mary was that unlikely person from an unlikely place whom God called for an unlikely purpose. Mary was the young lady who put literally everything on the line to please the Lord—her plans, her engagement, her reputation, her body, and ultimately even her life. The thing is, every Mary needs an Elizabeth, although sometimes it's hard to find one because some sisters have more seniority than spirituality. Elizabeth reminds us that a dream deferred is not a dream denied. Our significance need not be determined by what the world calls success, and we can trust God in the face of our shattered dreams. There will always be some people who don't believe in what God is trying to do in your life.

Notes

CHAPTER ELEVEN

When You Get Straightened Out

And He was teaching in one of the synagogues on the Sabbath. And there was a woman who for eighteen years had had a sickness caused by a spirit; and she was bent double, and could not straighten up at all. When Jesus saw her, He called her over and said to her, "Woman, you are freed from your sickness." And He laid His hands on her; and immediately she was made erect again and began glorifying God." — **Luke 13:10-13 (NASB)**

What should we do when we get straightened out? The more we read Scripture, the more we see how much we have in common with people who lived many centuries ago. They remind us so much of ourselves and our own life experiences. While they lived in a much simpler time and place, their issues were every bit as complicated as those we face today.

The woman in our text helps us to remember that at some point in life, we all have questions we can't answer, struggles we can't overcome, or problems we can't handle.

Some of us are dying from what we're eating. Others are dying because of what's eating us. For some, it may be an incident that happened in the past, but is now strangling our future.

We are told that the woman in our text was bent out of shape by a crippling infirmity that had been caused by an evil spirit. For eighteen years, she had been unable to straighten herself out.

Believe it or not, Satan is not intimidated by those who simply come to church—he's only intimidated when we come to Christ!

This woman teaches us two critical things about life. First, she teaches us what to do until we get straightened out. And then she teaches us what we ought to do after we've been straightened out.

Verse 10 is a portrait of this woman's resolution. For eighteen years she'd been debilitated by this infirmity, and yet she managed to make it to the holy place. It seems her condition had not hindered her commitment. She had a perfect excuse to stay away from church, but she went anyway.

Satan might have bound her physically, but he could not keep her out of church. What is even more interesting is that Satan didn't try to keep her out of church.

Believe it or not, Satan is not intimidated by those who simply come to church—he's only intimidated when we come to Christ! Satan has no problem with defeated people coming to church, because defeated people are usually trying to defeat other people.

During the most challenging days of her life, this woman's focus was on the Word of God.

Sometimes we think of the holy places, like the synagogue and the temple, as interchangeable. Both were central to Jewish life. But the focus of the temple was worship, while the focus of the synagogue was the Word.

There was worship in the synagogue, but it was all ancillary to the Word, since this was the teaching place. Verse 10 tells us Jesus was *teaching* in the synagogue.

During the most challenging days of her life, this woman's focus was on the Word of God. Running, jumping, singing, shouting, clapping, and dancing all have their place. But we need the Word to understand why we do these things.

We can learn a valuable lesson from a 1981 game of the San Diego Chargers. They were one of the best teams to ever *not* win the Superbowl. They ranked number one in offense out of 28 teams in the league at that time. They led the league in total offense, scoring 478 points and 6,744 total yards. But the problem was, the 1981 San Diego Chargers ranked only twenty-sixth out of twenty-eight in *defense*. What they taught the other teams was that offense sold tickets and drew crowds, but defense won championships.

The Word and worship are not matters of either/or. They must go together, just as offense and defense go together. Worship is like offense, but the Word is like defense. How tragic it is when a church ranks high in worship but low in the Word. Paul encourages believers to put on the whole armor of God.

> *Stand firm then, with the belt of truth buckled around your waist, with the breastplate of righteousness in place, and with your feet fitted with the readiness that comes from the gospel of peace.* — **Ephesians 6:14-15 (NIV)**

The reason we're defeated, delusional, and depressed is that we're all offense and no defense. We enjoy worship without internalizing the Word.

In Psalm 119 we read, "I have hidden your word in my heart that I might not sin against you," and "Your word is a lamp to my feet, a light on my path." Further down we read, "Direct my footsteps according to your word; let no sin rule over me" (Psalm 119:11; 105; 133, NIV).

According to Jesus Himself, "The Scriptures say, 'People do not live by bread alone, but by every word that comes from the mouth of God'" (Matthew 4:4, NLT). Moreover, "faith comes from hearing the message, and the message is heard through the word about Christ" (Romans 10:17, NIV).

It's okay to have some offense, but we need defense as well. Offense is great on Sunday, but we need defense between Sundays.

We need the Word inside us, because that Word can do more for us than whatever is happening on the outside. Let's keep our hands in the hands of the Lord, and hang in there. While verse 10 portrays the woman's resolution, verse 13 portrays her restoration.

Life was designed to be lived from the inside out.

Before she was straightened out, this woman's focus was on the Word. Afterward, her focus was on worship. For eighteen years, she had been incapacitated by an evil spirit that had rendered her incapable of raising herself up.

Maybe that's why she kept coming to church. She couldn't raise her body, but she could raise her spirit. That's really what peace is about—being cool on the inside when nothing is cool on the outside. It may be tough, but we know the Lord will keep us in perfect peace if our minds are steadfast and trust in Him (Isaiah 26:3).

Life was designed to be lived from the inside out. This woman couldn't raise her body, but she could raise her spirit. We are told in verse 10 that she had infirmity. But in the end she was "set free." This implies that the infirmity had *her*! So she was utterly helpless, but she was not hopeless. Have you been there? When your back was against the wall, did you look up and discover that "the one who is in you is greater than the one who is in the world" (1 John 4:4, NIV)?

Can you imagine what others might've called her? "Here she comes," people might have whispered, "that hunchback woman."

We might look helpless, but we go to church anyway, because we're not hopeless. The joy we feel on the inside doesn't come from the world; nor can the world take it away. Others can tear us down, but they can't steal our joy.

Look at what happened to this woman who was helpless but not hopeless. Jesus saw her, called her, spoke to her, touched her, healed her, and raised her. Isn't that our testimony too? He called her "Woman," which in that culture was a respectable term of endearment.

Can you imagine what others might've called her? "Here she comes," people might have whispered, "that hunchback woman."

But she wasn't a hunchback now, any more than "Blind Bartimaeus" was still blind, or the woman with the issue of blood was still bleeding.

Jesus told her, "Woman, you are set free from your infirmity" (Luke 13:12, NIV). In the Greek, the word used for "set free" is the same word as divorce. The Lord was saying, in effect, "You've been bound to Satan for eighteen years, but today I'm decreeing that you two are divorced. You can stay if you want, but he no longer has papers on you."

When we were lost in our sin, we were untouchable, but Jesus touched us anyway.

She no longer had to answer to the devil. Nor would she ever have to be set free again. It was done.

Another word picture in the Greek is of a gate that had been opened. In verse 12, the gate was opened, but she was not healed until verse 13. She was released before she was raised. Her plight before verse 12 was not her fault. But her situation after verse 12 was her responsibility. Some people today have been released but refuse to be raised. They can't see themselves beyond the reality they've come to know.

When we were lost in our sin, we were untouchable, but Jesus touched us anyway. He touched that woman and the Bible says she was immediately made straight.

It took her eighteen years to get there, but she did. What if she had quit going to church in the seventeenth year? What if she had quit after orientation? We must stick with church, come hell or high water. Oh, it gets a little rough now and then, but we must stay.

The greatest challenge for many of us is handling life in the interim—that time between the promise and the provision.

Once the woman was healed, she began to praise God. The word "praise" in the text is in the continuous tense, which means that once she started, she couldn't stop. It was as if she were saying, "I was sick for eighteen years, and now I feel like praising Jesus for the next eighteen hundred!" I can imagine her saying, "Just leave me alone, I'll turn out the lights when I'm through."

The greatest challenge for many of us is handling life in the interim—that time between the promise and the provision.

It doesn't matter how dark the day is. We have reason to rejoice. We can still say, "This is the day the LORD has made, and I have made up in my mind to rejoice and be glad in it" (Psalm 118:24).

The Apostle Paul said, "We are hard pressed on every side, but not crushed; perplexed, but not in despair; persecuted, but not abandoned; struck down, but not destroyed" (2 Corinthians 4:8-9, NIV).

Fanny J. Crosby was blind from early childhood, but during her life she wrote more than eight thousand hymns. They included "Close To Thee, I am Thine O Lord" and "Pass Me Not, O Gentle Savior." One hymn includes the following words:

Blessed assurance Jesus is mine;
O what a foretaste of glory divine!
Heir of salvation, purchase of God,
Born of his spirit, washed in his blood.[7]

Elsewhere she wrote:

Jesus, keep me near the cross,
There a precious fountain
Free to all, a healing stream
Flows from Calvary's mountain

In the cross, in the cross,
Be my glory ever;
Till my raptured soul shall find
Rest beyond the river.[8]

Even if we can't change our predicament, we can change our perspective. Fanny Crosby once told her mother, "If I had a choice I would choose to remain blind, because when I die the first face I'll ever see is the face of Jesus."

Chapter Eleven Questions

Question: In life we can have challenging days. Do you go to the Word of God to help you get through those days?

_____

_____

_____

_____

_____

_____

_____

_____

_____

_____

_____

_____

_____

_____

Question: Identify a past struggle. How did you overcome it? What did you learn?

_____

_____

_____

_____

_____

_____

_____

_____

_____

_____

_____

_____

_____

Question: What was the worst day or experience of your life? Read Psalm 118:24. Do you find worship to be therapeutic? Elaborate.

_____

_____

_____

_____

_____

_____

_____

_____

_____

_____

_____

_____

_____

_____

_____

_____

Summary: First, the bent woman teaches us what to do until we get straightened out. And then she teaches us what we ought to do after we've got straightened out. Believe it or not, Satan is not intimidated by those who simply come to church—he's only intimidated when we come to Christ! We need the Word inside us because life was designed to be lived from the inside out.

Notes

_____

_____

_____

_____

_____

_____

_____

_____

_____

_____

_____

_____

_____

_____

_____

_____

_____

_____

_____

_____

_____

References

1. Field, Richard "Dimples." *If It Ain't One Thing It's Another.* 1982.

2. Johnson, James Weldon. "Lift Every Voice and Sing." In *Complete Poems,* 109—110. New York: Penguin Group, 2000.

3. Martin, Civilla D. "His Eye Is on the Sparrow." In *Al Smith's Treasury of Hymn Histories,* edited by Al Smith. Greenville, SC: Better Music Publications, 1985.

4. Dunn, Deborah. "The SAM Syndrome: When Being Stupid Gets Really Serious." In *Stupid About Men,* 201—204. New York: Howard Books, 2009.

5. Crouch, Andrae. *Through It All.* 1993.

6. Shulz, Charles M. Schulz. *Peanuts.*

7. Crosby, Fanny J. *Blessed Assurance.* 1873.

8. Crosby, Fanny J. *Jesus, Keep Me Near the Cross.* 1879.

About the Author

Dr. R. Timothy Jones is married to the former Sherbrina Trammel and the father of three fine children: Timothy, Titus, and Mauri. He has been the pastor of the Peaceful Rest Baptist Church (The Family of Faith) in Shreveport, Louisiana since November 1994. The summer 2008 issue of *The African American Pulpit* cited Dr. Jones as one of "Twenty to Watch." He earned a Doctor of Ministry from Virginia Union University in May 2009, and is a former dean of the National Baptist Convention of America. He currently serves as president of the Baptist Missionary and Educational State Convention of Louisiana, and is a fellow of the Black Theology and Leadership Institute of Princeton Theological Seminary. One of his joys is teaching, as he is also an adjunct professor at Jarvis Christian College. Dr. Jones lives by three daily affirmations: *"To thyself be true, to God be faithful, and to others be kind."*

About SermonToBook.Com

SermonToBook.com began with a simple belief: that sermons should be touching lives, *not* collecting dust. That's why we turn sermons into high-quality books that are accessible to people all over the globe.

Turning your sermon or sermon series into a book exposes more people to God's Word, better equips you for counseling, adds credibility to your ministry, and even helps make ends meet during tight times.

John 21:25 tells us that the world itself couldn't contain the books that would be written about the work of Jesus Christ. Our mission is to try anyway. Because, in Heaven, there will no longer be a need for sermons or books. Our time is now.

If God so leads you, we'd love to work with you on your sermon or sermon series.

Visit www.sermontobook.com to learn more.